CW01022539

MICHAEL RUTTER
The Life of a Racer

Volume 2

Flesh and Blood

by

MICHAEL RUTTER
& JOHN MCAVOY

THE CHOIR PRESS

First published in the United Kingdom in 2022 by

The Choir Press

ISBN 978-1-78963-293-4

Picture Credits:

Philip Dranfield/PaintNation: Front Cover
Stuart Collins: Leather Suits
Double Red: Back Cover Image
Michael Rutter
John McAvoy
Tony Hall
Bauer Archive
Glynn Lewis

Contents

Thank You

I've no doubt that there are a lot of people who have got their own memories and stories about dad that we could have used in this book. He was 78 years old when he died, and he raced for thirty years, so he would have met hundreds if not thousands of people during his life. I am aware that for every one person who gave me their time to share their stories about dad for this book, there are probably a hundred others who could do the same.

It would have been impossible to get round everyone anyway, but as it happens, meeting people was tricky during the time we researched for this book due to the Covid pandemic. However, we reached a point where I feel all of dad's key moments in his life and career that I knew little or nothing about are covered thanks to everyone who helped me put this book together.

And of course, Juliette and Cecillia for putting up with me.

Dedication

2 minutes and 58.023 seconds is the exact time difference between mine and my dad's best laps of the Isle of Man TT course.

Dad set his in 1979, when he finished in second position in the Senior TT that year behind the late, great Mike Hailwood. His average speed over that lap was 112.32mph.

Mine was when I finished fourth in the 2017 Superstock race, and that lap was an average of 131.709mph.

There have been laps that I know were faster, but for some reason I didn't get to see them through due to being held up somewhere, and I'm sure Dad would say the exact same thing. That's the nature of us racers: we're never satisfied, it's never fast enough, it's never good enough.

Dad and I raced in completely different eras, which accounts for most of the time difference. I had a lot more power, grip, and in places the course is faster than it was in his day, so my best lap should be a lot faster than his, but I also have his DNA, which may or may not count for something.

Was it nature that decided I would follow in Dad's footsteps and become a racer? or was it because growing up in the race paddock while Dad raced was all I knew?

I've never really thought about this stuff until recently, when Mum and Dad both passed away. It has made me think a lot more about them now than I did when they were alive. Inevitably I see some of Dad's personality in mine and also some of Mum's softer side too, which I think probably means his lap on a bike with about half the power and half the grip of mine is probably a better one than mine. Who knows?

What I do know is that I want to share the stories I've been told about them, and my own that I can remember, as my tribute to them both. Most of them are about Dad, but like so many racers' wives and partners, Mum was never far away, looking after me and him, so she played a big part in Dad's life as a racer.

Neither of them got a decent funeral due to restrictions associated with the Covid pandemic, so this book is my tribute to them.

Tony Rutter, 29/4/41 – 24/3/20

Pauline Rutter, 03/03/43 – 07/02/21

Foreword

BY Carl Fogarty MBE

I'll be honest, I haven't had a lot to do with Michael over the years, but there was the time when according to him I emotionally wounded him after he asked me to borrow some tyre warmers at the Laguna Seca round of World Superbikes. I didn't recognise him, so said 'No', then left him standing there all alone and wearing a 'Foggy' T-shirt. There was also the restarted wet World Superbike race at Brands Hatch in 1997 that was being run on aggregate times. Michael passed me on track and disappeared up the road, but I left him to it as I wasn't racing him for the win due to him being so far back in the first, dry part of the race. Apparently, he still dines out on that pass, telling anyone who'll still listen all about it. Fair play to him, he was on it that day. At the time, he was at the start of his career – one that went on to be long and successful on the roads and short circuits, while I was a bit further into my career in racing.

Unlike me and Michael, our dads had much more to do with each other in the '70s and '80s, even becoming teammates for the 1982 Suzuka 8 Hour race on Dad's Ducati. I couldn't go on that trip, probably because I was doing exams at school or something, but I know Michael did go. He managed to get himself left behind all alone in a restaurant in downtown Tokyo by my dad and Tony, which caused a load of drama when they realised he was missing. My dad also bought a few race bikes from Tony, and my first race bike came from Tony too, so I know that as well as being competitors they did a bit of business over the years.

I know Dad had a lot of respect for Tony as a rider and rated him as one of the best. So, knowing there was a genuine friendship between him and my dad means that being asked to do the foreword for Michael's tribute to his father is lovely.

Michael and I followed in our dads' footsteps and also became bike racers. It might sound like something special, but if you think about it, kids growing up and doing what their parents do isn't that uncommon, even in the race paddock. Johnny Rea, Leon Haslam, William and Michael Dunlop, Guy Martin, Kenny Roberts Jnr, Remy Gardner and Valentino Rossi are just a few others who, like me and Michael, grew up going to race tracks every weekend to watch our dads race.

I remember how as a kid I'd be chucked in the back of the van to go all over the place with my dad – when I was younger it was Croft, Oulton Park or Aintree. As I got older I would go to places further from home with him, like the Isle of Man for the TT. To be fair that was my main memory of Dad – him racing there. He had some decent results at the TT, and a lot of bad luck too.

I was always getting into mischief in the hotel or the paddock, which wasn't far away. You could wander about anywhere you wanted back then and stand anywhere to watch the races. I would sit and dangle my legs over the bank at Signpost Corner and try to signal to Dad how he was doing in the race with a homemade pit-board. I used to get so into it that sometimes I would find it frustrating because I wanted him to do better than he did; he was my dad, and I wanted him to do well. In 1981 he was running fourth in a race, and I was desperate to try to let him know that he was two seconds up. It was a really close race and I loved the buzz of being involved, by trying to get the message across to Dad. It was the most important thing to me – plus it was a couple of weeks off school!

At school I struggled because I couldn't figure out why I was there. I knew what I wanted to do in life, so at secondary school, like Michael, I was thinking, what am I doing here? Lessons called Religious Studies, French and Science? I was like, what's the point? Then there were English lessons – I was like, what's that all about? I can speak English. None of it made any sense to me then, and the whole time I just wanted to race bikes and go and work for my dad; my pathway was already made out in my own little head at that age. Obviously it went on to be true and worked out alright, but it all started by loving going to the racing with Dad, just like Michael used to love going to the races with his dad, and missing school as much as possible!!

It was heaven; I used to go around on this little bike in the paddock and fields around Aintree and Oulton Park, and I'd just tear around. Then at Silverstone I found a bit of tarmac that was part of the old airfield I suppose, so I started going around on that, thinking it was a proper bit of the track. I've still got that bike to this day – a little 50cc three-speed Honda monkey bike, a funny-looking thing that had a straight-through exhaust, so I used to aggravate everybody because it was so noisy. Happy days.

Dad and his brother started their own business, just clearing yards and moving stuff about, pretty much anything to earn a few quid. Soon they got a truck so they could move more stuff about, then they ended up renting a warehouse and started doing haulage and storage, so the business got better and better. Dad's racing career was always a hobby; he was never professional like most people were then, including Tony. Dad never really had decent bikes, though to be fair, the ones he bought from Tony were very good. He got Tony's 1974 bike at the end of the season and raced it in 1975, and the same the year after, in 1976.

Tony's bikes must have been good because Dad did well enough on them to win some decent money, so next he bought Barry Sheene's bike from him in 1977 – God I wish he'd kept that bike; it even had 'Barry's Flyer' engraved on the engine. It was a 750cc triple that was really rare – even then. It was on that bike that Dad finished second to Joey at the TT in 1977 and had a good season that year – until he crashed and broke his skull at Aintree of all places, which was actually the second time he did that.

I remember the phone calls with Mum at home to tell us that he crashed at, of all bloody places, Carnaby Raceway, which was one of the safest circuits ever. Mum was on the phone, crying, and I was at her side asking if Dad was dead. She told me that he'd fractured his skull and was in hospital. It must have been coming up to Bonfire Night because when we visited him I asked if I could have a bonfire at home and he said, 'Yeah, no problem, just have it in the house.' I was like, Eh? What? As a kid, Dad getting hurt was so normal to me, and I didn't worry for him when he was out lapping the TT, or even when he was injured; I was more nervous for him not winning than anything else. I never thought for one minute that he could get killed, but when he told me to have a bonfire in the house, that freaked me out!

The bangs on Dad's head have affected him, and I know Tony suffered terribly later in his life due to the bangs he took on his head, and that was hard for Michael. Luckily, Dad isn't as bad and we're still able to take the mickey out of him to this day. He doesn't remember some stuff, and he has to write things down, even where he lives. He's got post-it notes all over his car with people's addresses and phone numbers – he's hilarious. He's moved to a remote place near Fleetwood, and as I write this, we're planning to meet up and get some dinner together somewhere. I've always been close to Dad, which is probably helped by the fact that bike racing was really a hobby for him and it never took over his life. Listening to the stories that Michael tells about his dad, it sounds like Tony was much more obsessed about winning than my dad was, which is probably why he doesn't have a lot of memories of doing stuff with his dad and why he's chosen to research and write this book.

Dad loved racing and he was good at it, but he wasn't as fussed about winning. For me it was all about winning. I remember during Dad's really good 1977 season – finishing second behind Joey at the TT and running second in the British Championship – there was a headline in Motorcycle News that read: 'George Fogarty – One of the nicest guys in racing'. He'd help anyone out and he just loved racing, especially going to Ireland and the Isle of Man to race; he loved the whole scene. He was different to me because, even as a kid, I'd get frustrated with him if he did a certain lap time at the TT. Once at the TT one of his mechanics didn't tighten up his back wheel properly, so his wheel came loose straight away, the chain came off his bike, and his race was over in a matter of yards. Another time, a mechanic put Dad's brake pads in the wrong way round when he set off with Mike Hailwood, so he had to pull over and stop. I was raging, but Dad wasn't; he was too nice. That said, in other ways if you're playing tennis or squash or even dominos with him, he's really competitive and gets fired up, just not at bike racing!

Like pretty much every kid that starts racing, Dad did help a lot in my early days, but it got less and less as I progressed, and when I eventually got signed by Ducati he would just come to certain races and make it a bit of a holiday for himself. But in the early days he was always there, helping me a lot doing this and that for me; it would have been difficult to do it without him, to be honest. I think Tony was more mechanically-minded than my dad, which I'm sure would have been a massive help to Michael, but then I guess as his career took off it might have been difficult for Tony to step back as Michael needed him less. My dad just left me to it, and only moaned when I crashed.

At the time, I didn't really care or think about if having my dad's surname made a difference. I just didn't see that it mattered because being in the paddock and around bike racing was so normal to me. I suppose being George Fogarty's son probably helped because he was an ex-racer and did well in his time, plus he was a nice guy in the paddock. I got a bit of free oil from Shell, some tyres from Michelin and some chains from Regina because of Dad's reputation. They were small things but important things that are difficult to get if you're an unknown. I've got no doubt that the Rutter name will have had the same benefit to Michael as the Fogarty name did for me, but it only goes so far. In the race paddock, if you don't get results, you'll soon get dropped, so trying to trade on your dad's name and reputation is pointless. You've got to stand on your own two feet pretty quickly or it'll all be over soon.

I probably wouldn't have been a racer if dad hadn't been one. I think whatever you get brought up around as a kid, the chances are you're going to do that. Motorbikes were there for as far back as I can remember, because Dad was racing. I do think that if he had done something else, the chances are I would have done that. I'll never know if that bug to race motorbikes would have come to me if Dad hadn't raced bikes. Probably not. Most of all, I'm just glad he raced motorbikes and didn't play cricket, because I'd have been shit at that!

I think the whole romantic idea of the son's destiny being to follow in their father's bike-racing footsteps is overthinking it a bit. Bottom line is that as kids we grew up around bikes and loved being around them, so it was completely normal to race them like our dads did. I'm pretty sure that most, or all, of what Michael went through with his dad, from going with him to all the race-tracks and spending days on end just messing about on bikes, to seeing him badly injured and suffering, then making his own way into bike racing, is the same as what every other son of a racer went through. That said, for every one of us who copied our dad and took up racing, there are probably a thousand or more who didn't. Obviously, Michael chose to race bikes like Tony, and he's still at it over thirty years later, which is about the same length of time Tony raced for, and you've really got to admit that's some good going for the both of them.

We were very sorry to hear of Tony's deteriorating health and eventual passing. He packed a lot into his life, some of it with my dad, including tales that I didn't know about until now, so while it's a shame that he's not here to tell his story himself, hats off to Michael for deciding to take the time and do it for him.

Carl Fogarty
March 2022

Introduction

2019 was a great year for me on and off the racetrack. I got a couple of podiums at the North West 200, I finished all five of the races I started at the Isle of Man TT in the top seven, which included another win in the TT Zero, and I won the Macau Grand Prix for the ninth time – in the most bizarre circumstances, but I'll still take it. The Bathams Racing team won races and came close to winning the National Superstock title with Taylor Mackenzie, and we even managed to pick up official support from BMW at the end of the season for 2020, which means they support us with bikes and engines. Then to round it all off we signed the rider that beat us to the 2019 title: Richard Cooper.

I also managed to publish a book without falling out with anyone, or at least as far as I'm aware! If you bought *The Life of a Racer* and are reading this, thank you. It must mean you enjoyed the first book, and I hope you enjoy this one just as much. Putting down all the things that I could remember at the time was a lot of fun, and the truth is that even while the first book was getting printed I was still remembering more stories, so this book's been inevitable for a long time, even before all the events of 2020 unfolded.

Pre-season testing in 2019 didn't go very well: We struggled to get Richard on the bike due to it arriving late and Richard's previous work commitments, but we did manage to get him on it for a day in Spain. Then he missed the first official test at Donington Park because Covid travel restrictions were introduced while he was in Spain, and he had to quarantine while the test took place. I did the testing and was shocked at how slow the bike was; it was something that would plague us for the whole season until the very last round.

Richard broke his leg at the first round and that was his and our championships over pretty much before they even started. It was a disaster. Then as the whole world was coming to terms with the sheer scale of the effect of Covid, it wasn't a big surprise when the North West 200 and the TT races were cancelled. In the space of a few weeks, our world had changed: we had a rider in hospital, a written-off bike that was also slow and no road racing.

Then Dad died.

It wasn't a massive surprise when Dad died – he'd been ill for a while – but it was still a sad time for me, and the reaction from the race paddock and fans was genuinely a surprise and very humbling. It's easy to forget just how long he had raced for and how successful he was, so to hear some of the tributes that were paid to him, and for the BBC to include him in the 'Remembering' bit of their Sports Personality show, was a really nice surprise.

My relationship with Dad was not typical at all. I never spoke to him about anything. He wasn't interested in talking about anything other than racing. Like I said in *The Life of a Racer*, I never talked to him about women, girlfriends, school or anything normal like that, but you know what? When he did talk, he was really interesting.

When he could still go to the pub with me, he would tell me a story about other racers, and I said to him, 'You never say anything about you', so he started telling me about him and his mates racing along the Stourbridge to Kingswinford road, a journey that today takes half an hour because of the traffic. He said he used to do it flat out on his Manx Norton, with his chin on the tank, like at a racetrack, because there was no traffic. Some of the stories were great, and I got more out of him in the pub atmosphere, just sitting there; I used to love listening to him. We were in Wordsley once, where he and I were brought up, and he recounted how back then no one cared about drinking and driving, and one day when he had just left the pub this policeman stood out in the road and stopped him. All the policeman did was tell him to drive himself straight home! Madness.

Now that he's gone, I realise now more than ever that I don't really know much about Dad. So, the reasons for this book are to keep telling my stories, but also for me to find out about my dad. I know some of it, but I don't know how much of what I know is myth, and how much is real. So, as well as more of my life as a racer, I've also been contacting people who raced against Dad, and people who were part of his life outside of racing; people who knew him better than I did. Talking to those people and learning more about the different sides to Dad made the end of 2020 much better than the beginning, and I hope you enjoy reading these tales as much as I did hearing them.

1
Giving Up

Dad's life as a racer ended in 1991 with retirement from the Supersport 400 race at the Isle of Man TT. The Suzuki he was riding was actually mine that I was using to do club racing on at the time. Its engine blew up during the race and left him sitting on the side of the road as a spectator while everyone else raced on. Just like that, his career as a racer – which had spanned thirty years, taken him around the world with all the highs, lows and adventures that you get in racing – was over.

Dad won four world championships and two British championships. He also won eight times at the Isle of Man TT, nine times at the North West 200 and five times at the Ulster Grand Prix, but despite having written his name in almost every history book that motorcycle racing has, it was on the 24th of March 2020 when, just like everyone else that ever lived, Dad's life eventually ended.

He had vascular parkinsonism and dementia, which meant, sadly for him, his life didn't end as abruptly as his career did. He spent most of the time between his career coming to an end and his last days wishing he could still be racing and wishing he could be at racetracks. It's all he ever wanted to do, right up to the very end.

The dual impact of Dad dying and 'normal' life stopping almost straight after due to the Covid pandemic has definitely made me stop and think about some things differently. I've had to stop and look around more. Racing has taken over my life just as it took over Dad's, which is something I've especially realised during this lockdown. It might sound stupid but being forced to stop and stay put by the lockdown has meant that I've seen stuff which I'd never seen before in my life, mostly to do with nature. For example, I've never seen birds build a nest, lay eggs in it and then see the chicks hatch and grow until 2020; it's blown my mind. I've even put a camera next to their nest and spent ages watching them; I've become obsessed. Also, I don't think I've ever seen any of the four seasons from start to finish, or at least that I've noticed. I usually go to Macau for the GP in November, and when I get back all the leaves from the trees have fallen while I've been away.

I've also never seen the first few months of the year because I'm away testing or something, so being sat at home for months reflecting on all these sorts of simple things has given me a really good bit of time to think about my future and realise that one day I will stop racing. Don't get me wrong: there have been days when it's been really depressing because it's felt like my life has just stopped. My life has been full of racing, and with that suddenly not happening it gave me little taste of what it must have been like for Dad after his accident: empty. One minute he's on top of the world, and the next it's all over for him; he never gave a thought to what he might do one day after he was done with racing.

There is something that the lockdown didn't change: mates would ring up and ask if I wanted to go to the pub, but I'd usually have to say I couldn't because I was away. During the lockdown, I had all the time in the world to be able to go out with mates, and we bloody couldn't because the pubs were all closed! No one could go out. The lockdown made me look at where I am with my racing career, and one thing I am sure of is that I still want to do as much as I can. I don't want to give up racing yet. I'd like to do the TT again; I love it, even if I will be fifty at the next TT in 2022. Having said that, I've got to be fit, and if I'm not fit, I won't do it. I'll also have to try and get myself back up to speed, maybe by racing in a support class, so I can have a half-decent go at the TT.

I've got a nice house, motorbikes coming out my earholes, financially I'm not rolling in it but I'm not skint either. I've got everything I ever dreamed of, and more. But I'll still sit on the sofa and look out at my garden and think, 'What's it all about? Is this it?' I've been doing something with such a high level of intensity for so long that even though I've had a glimpse of what life after racing might be like, and plenty of thinking time to prepare for it, I still know it's not going to be an easy adjustment to make. That's the thing about elite sport: you have to stop relatively young not just because it's so demanding, but also because you're a long time retired, and you have to fill that time with something or you'll go out of your mind. It's no good going back and competing at club level to get a fix because it won't be the same; it can't be the same once you've been around the world and raced at the very highest level.

Me and John McGuinness were talking the other day and wondering what we are going to do. We have lived the dream, and the truth is we still are, but it is 100% going to stop for us, and it will be because of an accident or because we can't physically do it anymore; we're also not quick enough these days, and to be honest I'm nearly at that point now. It is really depressing and so hard to accept. The best thing for me would be one day to just wake up and not want to do it anymore, to wake up and be scared of it, then just do something else.

Unlike Dad, I do like doing DIY jobs around the house and taking on projects. I built a shed recently and even though everyone takes the piss because I'm not great at it, I don't care because I like making stuff, and I enjoy it. I like the social side of DIY too; I think if you can get a lot of mates involved it can be a right laugh, but the problem is most of them have all got regular jobs.

Dad was useless at DIY and once got my mate Scott to do some work on his car for him; he wouldn't even do that himself. Scott told me that at one point Dad got him to do some work on the cylinder head for him. Scott phoned Dad and told him that the cylinder head bolts were stretch bolts, which means they stretch every time you torque them up, so you're only supposed to use them once and then replace them the next time. Apparently, Dad just said, 'Ahh, bloody hell, just bloody put those ones back in, Scott. They're all right.' Scott explained that they could snap if he did that and he might have to take the whole thing apart again if that happened, but Dad was adamant and told him to just do it. As Scott was torquing up the bolts, he could feel one about to snap, so he just ignored Dad's instructions and got some new bolts. Later, when Scott was telling the story to Mum and Dad at home, Dad would not accept that he was wrong, and started giving Scott a hard time for not wanting to reuse the old bolts!

The thing is, as a racer, it's really easy to think of stopping racing as the end, but in reality, it isn't. It's just the end of that era. Being too old to race competitively doesn't mean you're too old to do other things. But how do you fill that gap? I don't think Dad did.

He spent his later years just wishing he could still be racing and never accepted that nothing lasts forever, and you just can't do that; it'll wear you down.

There's a bloke at the local DIY shop who knows me through bike racing. It seems everyone knows me there because I'm there so much these days with all the jobs around the house that I'm finally getting round to doing. This bloke must be about seventy and he only works a few days a week there, and he's so knowledgeable and so good with people. He always asks me how the racing is going and all that, and I think that's me now, but with the racing; doing a bit less and a bit less until I finally stop. I look at that bloke in the DIY shop and think he obviously had a career before he started working there, but he's as happy as a pig in shit, helping bodgers like me muddle our way through various projects. He's got it right and, like him, I want my next chapter and later years to still be fun and interesting.

I've been trying to keep on top of my financial stuff. Obviously, with my racing coming to an end my earning capacity is falling, but luckily I've put some aside in pensions and things like that. My financial adviser asked me what is the most important thing that I want to spend my money on, and after virtually a whole day of talking to him about my priorities and things like that, he worked out in the end that the big thing for me is health, so I can actually do stuff and enjoy it. I could have all the money in the world, yet if I can't enjoy it, there's no point.

I'd like to own a pub and do it out how I'd like it, but I'd like someone else to run it. I'd still like to be involved in motorbikes because that's been my life and I enjoy it – maybe testing for manufacturers or tyre companies, or more magazine work. I'll keep doing the classic racing for sure and keep Bathams Racing going and basically do what Dad didn't do: keep busy. It's strange because something Dad did teach me was to not just do one thing but do lots of different things in bike racing – to keep busy and always have a plan B. He did road racing, the TT, short circuits, endurance racing, British championships, world championships – you name it, he raced it – but the irony is that outside of racing he didn't use the same logic. He didn't have a clue what to do with himself, or a backup plan.

I think Dad gave up and really went downhill when he started to lose his ability to get about; his independence was his life. For the last couple of years of his life, he was stuck in a chair, which was about the worst thing you could do to him. He had dementia too, and when I visited him at the care home he'd ask if his car was outside and stuff like that. I decided it was easier to just go along with it. It was sad to see, especially after what he achieved, ending up in a care home. Don't get me wrong: they were great at the care home, and I know Dad wasn't the easiest person to look after, but it was his idea of hell. It made me look at my life a bit more and think, wow, you've got to enjoy it while you can. I think he definitely enjoyed his life when he was able to, just like we said in the eulogy at his funeral: my dad got up in the morning and did exactly what he wanted, and he got away with murder!

It was really quick between when Mum went into the care home and when Dad went in. I think people who have had to arrange getting one or both of their parents into a care home understand that it's hard enough anyway, you know, making that decision to have someone else take over caring for your parents on your behalf. But on top of that, I was racing and setting up the Bathams Racing team, and things that most people would find simple, like all the forms that you have to fill in, was hard for me because of my dyslexia. I found the whole process really difficult.

Mum had to go into the home about a year before Dad. It's difficult to talk about, and I've never really shared any details about my mum. Dad's low mood was brought about by being forced to give up due to his physical health, but Mum had her own mental health issues. She had suffered from paranoid schizophrenia for as long as I can remember, so she thought people are out to get her. In the house we could only have blunt knives because she would think someone was going to kill her. Her symptoms were pretty extreme compared to the average person with the condition. It's truly a terrible thing, and certainly nowadays the professionals know a lot more about it than they did back when Mum first started suffering from it. Apparently, one in a hundred people suffer from it in some form.

One day it got too much for Mum. I went round to see Mum and Dad, and when I went into the house Dad was sitting on the sofa and turned around to me and said, 'Michael, I haven't seen your mum. She's gone missing.' I asked Dad how long she had been missing for, and since at that time he was having to sleep on the sofa downstairs because of his injuries, he knew that she'd left the house at 2 a.m., and it was now about three in the afternoon. I said, 'What do you mean she's gone?', and he said that she'd just left in the middle of the night.

Mum had said to me before that she wanted to end it, that she wanted to commit suicide, so I was really worried, and I went off, running around the area near their house looking for her. Up the road from their house there is a canal, so I went there, but there was no sign of her. I tried to think where she could have gone because her shoes were gone but her jacket wasn't, so I searched all the places nearby that I thought she might be.

Eventually, I thought I should go back home and call the police. They asked me where I thought she would have gone, and I told them that I hadn't got a clue and that I'd just been out looking for her nearby. I told them that I thought I should notify them just in case they could help. Then I decided to call a few of her friends, and none of them had seen her. As I was doing that, I was looking out the window and saw the garage door open. My heart sank and I thought to myself 'Oh no' and ran outside. The door was only slightly ajar, but straight away I could see that Mum was in the garage, just lying there. She was unconscious but still alive, so I pulled her out and called for an ambulance, which arrived really quickly and took her to hospital.

Mum had taken an overdose. She had a couple of bottles of tablets because she was on loads of medication for all her problems, and that night she just fired them all in.

At the hospital, the doctors were saying that Mum was in a really bad way, and they asked whether I wanted them to try and revive her. The thing is, up until about a month before this happened, she had been a lot better and was looking after herself. She'd been in and out of a home for mental illness but she'd seemed to have got over the worst of it, so I didn't know why she had suddenly decided to try and take her own life. So, I said to the doctors that of course I wanted them to revive her, because she had been fine lately. Sometimes I think that was a mistake on my part, especially because when she did come round from it all and was normal again, she said to me directly that if I ever saw her like that again to just leave her.

Mum came home about Christmas time and then soon after she had to go back into hospital because she started going downhill again. She was really well for about a month, and it was during that month that she told me do not to do that again. She wasn't cross with me for doing it, but I did feel guilty for telling the doctors to try and revive her. In hindsight, sometimes I think I should have left her, but not in the state that I found her, on the garage floor; that's a shitty place for it to end.

The doctor said Mum was really ill. On top of her mental problems, she also had physical problems because all the tablets had damaged her kidneys to the point where she needed dialysis. Her body had pretty much shut down and she'd been like that for three years. I mean, what was the best thing for her? What quality of life did she have now, all because I asked the doctors to help her? She just sat in a white room with no view. It's tragic, and I felt so sorry for her, but then again, that's life I suppose. I don't know if I'd have carried a load of guilt if I'd told the doctors to leave her and let her slip away, but I know now that it was an impossible question to answer. Whatever I did, I couldn't do the right thing. You can only do what you think is right at the time.

Mum never really came out of hospital after that; she went into a home, and in no time at all Dad went into the same home. At the time, I had just started racing in superstock, so it would have been 2016. Once or twice during that season, I'd had to leave the circuit to try and help Mum because she'd got herself all worked up; they were hard times. I'd be lying if I said I wasn't worried that I was going to get the same illness as Mum – you know, you follow your family. But I think you have got to have some guts to try and kill yourself, or you've got to be seriously unwell and in a really bad place. The only thing I've got going for me that I didn't get from Mum and Dad is that I can take the piss out of myself, which helps. Mum died on the 7th of February 2021.

I think it's something to do with the local sense of humour that we have in the Black Country, but the other day someone was asking how's it going, and I said, 'Suicidal.' I think it must have shocked them because they started asking if I'd planned it. I said, 'Oh yeah, of course I have. I'm going start all my bikes up in the garage, including the RCV on half throttle, and sit on a chair in the middle of them all, and either I'll die, or they'll run out of petrol.' This person said, 'Bloody hell. Make sure you call me first. Don't do that.' So then I had to make sure he knew I was only joking! The bottom line is that I haven't got the balls to kill myself.

Giving up isn't easy. Mum obviously reached that point after a really long struggle with her mental health, and Dad was forced to give up racing when he didn't want to. His body just couldn't do it anymore, especially after his crash at Montjuic Park in 1985, but his mind wouldn't accept it, and it made him really frustrated in his old age. At the time of writing this book, the 2021 TT and North West 200 have been confirmed as cancelled, with no word yet on the Macau GP, so for all I know even though in my mind I haven't given up racing, it's possible that without knowing it, my race at Brands Hatch in Dad's colours was my last competitive race, and the 2019 Macau GP was my last race win.

2
From Nobody to Somebody

Since Dad passed away, I've learned so much more about him. As I said before, we never really spoke about much; all he was bothered about was motorbikes, so I never really knew much about his life outside of that. At his funeral, I got talking to two guys that I never even knew existed and who, as it turned out, were lifelong friends of Dad's who went to school with him and were also visiting him at the care home right up to the end. I couldn't resist spending an afternoon with Bob Kitson and Keith Wheeler to try and find out more about Dad's early years, and they did not disappoint.

Dad was a year older than Keith and lived a mile from where he did. They first met at school, when they were eleven and twelve years old. Keith says that Dad wasn't very outgoing at school; he was very quiet and all they really did was chase one another around the playground. Away from school, they would play in a local scrapyard that scrapped old Spitfire planes. When he left school at fifteen, Keith got a job in a factory as an apprentice, and on his first day he bumped into Dad, who'd left school the previous year and who was now working on a lathe at the same factory. The factory was Fry's Diecasting in Wordsley, which manufactured engine cases for Royal Enfield motorbikes. Dad and Keith didn't understand why they painted them red on the inside, only to find out later that the paint was to cover holes!

Bob was from Smethwick and didn't meet Dad and Keith until 1960, when he was riding his motorbike along the Stourbridge-to-Bridgnorth road, known locally as just 'the Bridgnorth road', and about three or four bikes went past him. He tried to keep up but couldn't until he got to Bridgnorth, where he found Keith, Dad and another bloke called John Richardson. The four of them just hit it off, and it sounds like the four of them were a right bunch of tearaways. According to Keith, they used to go to a café in town and look for fights with lads from the nearby RAF base Stanmore. The RAF lot were all perfectly turned out with their hair all full of Brylcreem, whereas Dad and his mates were just the local greasy bikers. This was around 1959/60, so Dad would have been about eighteen years old. The other thing about the café that they went to was that there was a reaction machine that tested your reflexes: you'd put a penny in the top and there was a handle that suddenly released the penny and you had to see how quickly you could stop it. Bob reckons nobody could beat Dad, that his reactions were easily the best.

They had an afternoon in the police station in Kingswinford once. That day they had met at the bottom of a hill on the Bridgnorth road before going into town. John reckoned his Norton Dominator was getting quicker for some reason, so they all took turns to

Me and Dad.

Sat with mum. The less said about my haircut, the better.

Just a really nice picture of mum.

Mum and Dad at the TT.

fantastic collection of pictures that show Dads journey from a small child to being the toast of the TT.

The famous dead heat between Dad and Ray McCullough at the 1977 North West 200.

Dad with his engine tuner Fred Hagley (centre) and Professor Gordon Blair from Queens University Belfast, who tuned Ray McCullough's engine in the dead heat. They had a lot of mutual respect.

Dad on one of his Yamahas wearing Honda leathers.

...ads first podium at the
...T in 1972 alongside
...gostini.

1979 Senior TT podium. Mike
Hailwood won, Dad was second
and did his best ever lap of the
TT and Dennis Ireland was
third. Hailwood was even brilliant at spraying champagne.

There are lots of jumps at the TT.

I loved my Scalextric track. Little did I know that years later they would make a model of me that you could buy.

Just a collection of fantastic photos that capture the atmosphere and amount of fans that there were at road racing in Ireland in Dads day. It's still the same today.

have a go on it, up and down the road, to see what he was on about. The next day the police came round and took Dad to the police station, and when he got there, Keith and John were already there. Somebody had reported that some lunatics were racing up and down the Bridgnorth road doing all sorts of dangerous manoeuvres. They were in there for five hours while Dad said it was Keith's fault, Keith said it was John's fault and John said it was Dad's fault, which strictly speaking was all true. In the end, the police just let them go and told them not to let it happen again. That sort of thing didn't bother Dad. Keith said that sometime after the police warned them to behave, they had been going so fast on the same road that they stopped at a barn at the end of the road, leaned the bikes up against it and pissed on the brakes to cool them down – just as a coach full of school-children went past. It didn't bother Dad one bit.

Keith told me that there was another brush with the law when they were riding out to the White Harte pub in Kinver, as they often did. On one occasion John took Dad's Royal Enfield because his chain had broken and Dad said he had a spare link at home. Keith said he'd take Dad home to get the link, and Keith had his missus with him too, so there was three of them on the bike. Inevitably they rode right past a police van, so the next time they were at the White Harte, the police sergeant showed up and announced that he had seen Dad three-up on a bike and that he was going to arrest him. Just like before, they just all blamed each other and got away with it!

Bob and Keith remarked on how Dad was pretty unflappable and rarely lost his temper. This was something I already knew, but I was surprised to hear a story from Bob that ended up with Dad in a canal with his pushbike. He was seeing a girl called Fran Mackenzie who lived in Wordsley, on a street joined to the canal via an alleyway. One Sunday morning Dad said to Bob to come over on his pushbike and they'd all have a ride down the canal to Stourport to watch someone else they knew doing some scrambling – what's known as Motocross today. So, Bob met John at Dad's, went on to Fran's then went down the alleyway to the canal. Fran, who was in front, suddenly stopped dead because someone was coming towards her. Everyone behind her stopped in time – except for Dad, who ended up in the canal. So much for the bloke with lightning reflexes. They helped Dad out of the canal, and he jumped back on his bike, cycled home to change and caught everyone up at the scramble.

Before Dad started racing bikes himself, he and his mates were always following it. Five of them went to Silverstone one year in an Austin Cambridge that some fella let them have for the weekend. It sounds like they were all lucky to get there and back alive because Bob said he remembers thinking it was cold in the back of the car and lifted the carpet to investigate a drought and he could see the road! The floor of the car had rotted right through.

The friends used to go to Wolverhampton to have their hair cut. It might seem a long way to go for that, but there was this place on Worcester Street, in some vaults underneath the cinema that they always went to. In the vaults there were two or three barbers, but at the end there was a curtain, and they found out that if you paid a bit more you could go behind it, and a young topless lady would cut your hair. Can you imagine such a thing these days? Having said that, they could never afford the extra, so they only went there on the off-chance of getting a glimpse!

They didn't always get along though, and Keith wanted to tell me about the time he and Dad had a massive fight. On Saturday mornings at the workshop at Fry's Diecasting, everyone had to clean their machine and work area. There was a bit of cloth that some of the lads would soak in slurry and chuck about, and while you'd be working away and not looking, the cloth would smash you straight in your earhole. This went on until eventually Dad lost his temper after one of the other workers scored a direct hit on his face. Dad turned around and thought it was Keith, so he marched over and grabbed hold of him and started trying to punch him. Eventually, the foreman stepped in and told them to pack it in or they'd get the sack. He told them that they'd be finished work in an hour so could carry on then if they wanted, so that's what they did. Apparently the first five minutes was just them saying, 'Go on, you hit me', 'No, you hit me', 'No, you throw the first one' until eventually one of them got fed up and went for it. They spent the next forty-five minutes punching one another and rolling around on the floor until some of the people watching told them to pack it in and shake hands. Keith thinks Dad knew it wasn't him who threw the cloth, but he wouldn't say; he'd made his move and saw it through. Keith says he went home and started to cry, and when his mum asked why he was crying, he said, 'I just fell out with my best mate.' Luckily, they put it behind them and they went on to be lifelong friends.

Dad got his first bike when he was 16, and it was a BSA B35 350cc that Keith and Bob describe as a bit of a hack. It's nice to know that nothing changes; most people's first bike is usually a bit rough. They never had field bikes or things like that, so went straight onto the road. His next bike was a maroon 250cc Royal Enfield Clipper, which I'm told was beautiful but not that fast, so it didn't last long. Bob said that he and Dad would go on his Royal Enfield to the Royal Enfield factory at Redditch during their lunch break. They had an hour for lunch so would sneak out five minutes early and go from work at Wordsley to the factory, go to the spares department, get what they needed and get back to work as quick as they could. They could never get back in time and were usually ten minutes late, so they would have to sneak back in, hoping nobody noticed.

After the Royal Enfield, Dad bought a Norton Dominator, which he took to the TT in '61 or '62. Keith and Bob didn't go, but Dad went with another lad that knew called Clive Horton, who I'm sure also came to his funeral. That trip was a big deal for Dad, and it's not a surprise that Keith and Bob reckon that's when Dad got the TT bug. Soon after that trip, they started going up to see a local fella called Gerald Underwood for some advice on how Dad could go about starting to race.

Gerald raced a BSA 350 Goldstar, and Dad was keen on getting a Goldstar to replace his Dominator, so he and Bob would go to Gerald's and hang about in his 8ft x 5ft shed maybe twice a week, every week. Gerald would get them to help out with odd jobs on his race bike such as polishing and cleaning it until eventually the effort paid off. When Gerald decided he wanted a 350 Norton instead, he gave Dad first dibs on his Goldstar. Gerald put the lights back on it for Dad and all the electrics so he could ride it on the road. That was the bike Dad started racing on, so it was only on the road for a short while. Bob reckons that Dad got clocked at 117mph at Aintree on that Goldstar, which is bloody quick; it must have had a really strong engine. When Dad first got that Goldstar, he and Bob would ride their bikes to Mallory Park so he could buy some part-worn race tyres. Bob would carry one around his shoulder and Dad carried the other. The tyres were only £3 for a set, which explains a lot about what I'll do for a bargain!

After Dad bought that Goldstar from Gerald, he took it to Oulton Park with Mum to watch Gerald race. When the racing finished,

Mum, Dad and Bob went back to their bikes, and the carburettor had gone from Dad's Goldstar. Someone had just snipped through the cables and pulled it off the bike, so the organisers put out an address over the PA system asking if anyone could take a bike back to the Wolverhampton area, and sure enough one of the competitors offered to put it in his van and take it back, and gave Mum and Dad a lift too. Bob jumped on his bike to ride home on his own but stopped when he noticed something loose. He found that the side panel on his bike was hanging loose and all the tools that lived in the compartment behind it had gone. The thieves had used Bob's tools to pinch Dad's carburettor.

Bob said that Dad was always that much quicker on the road than anyone else but that his whole interest in racing started with Gerald, just standing in his shed, listening to him telling them stories of his racing. It was also Gerald that gave Dad his first bit of advice on how to start racing – to get a licence and join a club. So, Dad, Bob and John joined the Midland Motorcycle Racing Club, which met up every week at the Red Lion pub in Handsworth. I looked up some pictures of the pub to see what it looks like, and it looks amazing, or at least it looks like it was amazing. It's been empty for some time now and fallen into disrepair, but you can see the architecture is still there and imagine what it must have been like back then with all those people meeting there once a week. They used a room upstairs above the bar and all they did was talk motorbikes – heaven!

The club used to run sprints at Prees Heath, Pirton and Church Lawford. Church Lawford was actually a timed lap instead of a timed straight one-way run up a hill or something: they had a bus with some timing gear inside it, so you started in front of the bus, then went around some corners and back down the runway past the bus. It wasn't a race as such because that's the point of a sprint: it's you against the stopwatch, and the fastest in their class was the winner. Apparently, Dad always used to do well at Pirton and Prees Heath until about '63/'64, when people started using Hondas, which were new and much faster and wiped the floor with everyone. It didn't take long for Dad to find his way to Aintree, where there's a proper racetrack, for his first race rather than a sprint, and so began his life as a racer.

I love the stories that Bob and Keith told me about those very early days going around with Dad and his Goldstar. They remind me a lot of my early days, when there's virtually no pressure and it's still a hobby. There's one anecdote that stands out and sums up what it's like for all racers starting out, when the whole thing is just a massive adventure. It's a great story now, but it could have been the end for them all before it even began.

Dad's van was a Morris J2 Drifter with a flat front. It was tiny and the engine was inside the front between the driver and passenger seat. Dad and his mates all went to Oulton Park, along with another local bloke called Roger Cartwright, who raced a Norton Dominator. Thanks to Roger's Dominator and Dad's Goldstar, the van only had a top speed of about 40mph, so they got nowhere fast. That was the Saturday, and their plan for the Sunday was to go to Snetterton, so after the racing had finished at Oulton Park, they packed up the tiny van with the two bikes and five people altogether and started the 200-mile overnight drive between the two tracks. I've looked up pictures of those vans and I have no idea how it accommodated five people, two bikes, tools and spare parts.

They got as far as King's Lynn in Norfolk before the van broke down, so they never made it to Snetterton. They managed to get it fixed, but it took all day on the Sunday to sort, so they decided to just head for home via the A47, which would take them all the way to Leicester. At some point they spotted an old tramp sitting on the side of the road. Everyone else said there wasn't any room to pick someone up, but Dad insisted. The tramp got in the back, and according to Bob he absolutely stank. About four miles later, the van got a puncture and Dad lost control of it and went through a hedge and down an embankment. It rolled three or four times but by some sort of miracle it landed on its wheels. Bob woke up next to Roger in the middle of a field because the back doors had been flung open and they had been thrown from the rolling van.

The whole of the van was a twisted wreck with steam coming from everywhere; it was a mess. They looked around for the tramp and found him about 50 yards away from where they ended up. He was OK, and he was just sitting there holding his wrist, but he was covered in cow shit from his backside up to the top of his head. The poor sod survived a massive car accident but must have landed in a big cowpat and slid through it. When you're down on your luck, you're down on your luck. Before they got the police, they had a whip-round and gave the tramp some money, and he disappeared, never to be seen again.

The crash happened at a place called Houghton on the Hill, and this was when most villages had a police house. Houghton on the Hill's police house just so happened to be next to a scrapyard, so the van got scrapped on the same day. A farmer had to pull the van from the field to the scrapyard, and the friends got a bus home. Bob had blood tricking out of his head, one of the other guys had blood coming out of his ear, the tramp looked like he'd broken his wrist and got covered in cow shit, yet Dad didn't have a hair out of place! They remember Dad getting a bill for £3.75 for putting a massive gap in the farmer's hedge, but nobody can remember how Dad got his and Roger's bikes home. They'd left them at the police house, and they must have hired a van and gone back for them. But anyway, there they all were, battered, bruised and bleeding (except for Dad), getting a bus to Leicester, then another bus from Leicester to Birmingham, then a taxi to Wordsley. They got home well past midnight and went back to work the next morning. What a weekend, what an adventure and what a lucky escape for everyone. Soon after that, Dad traded in his Goldstar for a Norton 350, which was another step up in performance.

I can't remember much about my Granddad, but obviously at this time Dad was still living at home, so it was great to hear from Bob and Keith that they remember him and the house. All I remember about him is he was miserable and always having a go at my nan. He smoked a pipe all the time, his garden was perfect, and he had a brilliant woodworking shed. According to Bob, he was really into his gardening and didn't really get involved in Dad's racing. They lived on Graham Road in Kingswinford and there was a lean-to shelter on the side of the house where Dad kept his bike, and whenever they were fettling it, they'd go there and spend hours under that lean-to while Granddad spent most of his time in the garden. Across the street lived a fella who was an engineer by trade who had a shed with a milling machine, a lathe, polishing machines and all sorts of engineering tools, so whenever they wanted anything doing, they'd go over there and ask him for help. He was really old-school and went everywhere in his leather engineer's apron. Bob said that when Granddad died, Dad didn't say a lot to his mum and kept himself to himself, so whenever Bob went around, he'd get the third degree from Nan about what Dad was up to. Then Nan found out that Bob's wife had her hair done in one of the shops opposite where Dad lived, so Nan started going there to get her hair done and got all the information on Dad she wanted.

There was another bloke who Dad and his mates used to hang about with called Barry Randle. He was well into his bikes too, and like Dad, he had ideas of doing some racing, which became a bit of a thing between them. Barry left the area when he was ten, then came back when he was sixteen and just slotted straight back in and worked in the local paper shop. Every Wednesday Bob and Dad used to go over to Barry's paper shop and buy a copy of Motorcycle News and Motorcyclist magazines, one each that they'd swap after they had read them. When Barry got a racing licence and entered a race, apparently Dad was properly angry because Barry had entered a race before him. It was the first sign of a competitive streak in Dad that maybe even he didn't realise he had until he experienced not being the first to do something racing-related.

Barry also did the TT before Dad and finished second to Phil Read in the 250cc race and third to Agostini in the 500cc race, so Barry was no slouch. At Mallory Park he and Dad were virtually unbeatable, always qualifying for the final on a grid of riders that included people like Mike Hailwood, but Barry's career was a lot shorter than Dad's. Bob always classed Dad as a '1, 2, 3 finisher' and Barry as a '3, 4, 5 finisher'. Bob still has the programmes from those races at Mallory Park, and the winner of the heats got £3, second got £2 and third got £1. In the final the winner got £15, which was big money at the time.

Barry got an entry to race at Monza, When Bob went to the paper shop Barry told him that an entry to a race had come through, but he couldn't understand it because it was all in Italian. Luckily, Bob knew a bloke in the foundry who sang Italian opera and who would surely be able to help. He arranged to meet the bloke with Barry in the phone box opposite his shop during this guy's ten-minute break. He took one look at all the Italian and said he couldn't understand a word of it and that he just learned words of the opera and sang them without knowing what any of them meant. Naturally Dad was devastated that Barry was the first to race on the continent and he sulked for at least two days apparently, but like everyone else he was pleased for Barry when he finished the race second to Jarno Saarinen. At the time Saarinen was a high-profile Grand Prix rider from Finland who would be 250cc world champion in 1972 and runner-up in the 350cc class in the same year. Sadly, he died in an accident in 1973 at Monza, so for Barry from the paper shop to go to Italy and beat everyone except him was a big deal.

After about five years, around '66/'67, Bob says that Dad was getting quite a clique around him and the entourage of followers got bigger and bigger when Dad would go to the Queen's Head, which was their local pub in Wordsley. Meanwhile, Barry was racing on his own most of the time. The only help he had was if his wife Janet went with him, but most of the time Barry preferred Janet to stay at home and run the shop. Bob stepped back a bit from Dad at that point to help Barry. In 1975 at Silverstone Barry had a nasty accident that really damaged his ankle. He never got the movement back, so he packed it in and took up golf and just disappeared. He had nothing to do with Dad or anyone from the group for several years.

Bob wasn't the only one to find himself pulled away from Dad. Keith couldn't afford to keep up with Dad's constant travelling and racing every weekend, so he went scrambling with John. John bought a Cotton Quest in kit form, built it in Keith's kitchen and went racing the next day. He took to it like a duck to water and won his first race in "Experts," so got moved into Seniors and won that too. John talked Dad into buying a 250 Suzuki to have a go, but halfway through Dad's first meeting he said, 'No thanks, not for me' and never did it again. John also did the same to Barry and got the same response. Three guys that all lived within a mile of each other – John, Dad and Barry – and they all turned out to be top racers.

As Bob said, by the late sixties Dad already had a following locally, and he reckons Dad influenced a lot of local bikers to have a go at racing. Maybe they only did one or two meetings, and a lot would have packed it in, unable to afford it, but Bob is adamant that for a while nearly every single one of them that had a go could be traced back to Dad's influence and popularity in the area. Another factor was that the Queen's Head pub was right next to a haulage firm owned by a bloke called Bob Priest, who was into his bikes and who saw what was going on with Dad. Bob Priest was Dad's first proper sponsor in 1968, and the sponsorship opened up a whole world of possibilities for Dad when it came to machinery and engine tuners, and that's the point at which things really took off for Dad. Bob isn't sure exactly how Dad and Bob Priest got together but says that he was a very big influence on Dad.

Those early years of Dad's racing career sound like they were just typical of any racer's first few seasons – just doing it for the fun of it and with a group of mates. The sixties was a very different time to be alive: the world was a much, much bigger place, and even though the things they did to entertain themselves seem so harmless and innocent compared to today, there is no question that Dad was very lucky to have had such a brilliant group of like-minded friends around him, as even though it's obvious that Dad was the quickest rider of the gang, he wasn't the quickest to the bar. Even so, Bob very generously says that he grew up with Dad and never once thought of him as selfish. A tight bugger? Yes, but that's not the same. Bob would get the first drink then Dad would get the second, then Bob the third and while he was at the bar, Dad would get him to buy some pork scratchings too, then declare that he'd had enough and it was time to go home! It was also during those years that Dad met Mum in a café at Halesowen where all the bikers would go for a coffee. Dad, Bob and Keith had ridden out there, as they did, and Mum was there too. She didn't work there; she was just there with her group of friends, and the rest is, as they say, history.

Bob Priest would talk Dad and his mates into going over to a club on Canal Street – there would be about twelve of them altogether. Bob Priest would get a round of drinks for everyone and then one of Barry's sponsors would get a round of drinks in, and all the time Dad would be shrinking into the background and would eventually ask Bob if he wanted to go halves on a round of drinks. Of all the stories Bob and Keith told me about Dad, that one is the least surprising.

As Bob and Keith say, they drifted away from Dad for a few years as Dad's career took off, but when it was all over, the three of them reconnected again and got back on their bikes to have more adventures, which I'll get to later on in the book.

3
Behind Every Great Racer

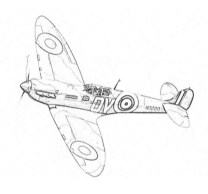

The idea of it being impossible to succeed at the highest level of our sport on your own is a cliché, but it's also true. You need a good team in the garage, good sponsors and good equipment. There are plenty of people these days who will say that you can't be competitive on a modern bike unless you've got an electronics whizz-kid with a laptop, and that is true. I'd be the first person to agree with that, as we found out to our detriment at Bathams Racing in 2020 and 2021. We got lost with the electronics on the BMW we raced then, and despite having two of the very best riders for those seasons, they and we got nothing like the results that we were all capable of. Once we got on top of the electronics the bike was transformed and we were instantly back at the front, racing for wins again.

The thing is, though, that the very same could be said about

Dad's era of racing. Obviously, there were no electronics then, but there was a lot of potential in the engines that not all tuners could extract, and if you wanted to win, you had to get your engine tuned. Nowadays the engines are so good and so powerful that they just need looking after with the same sort of maintenance you do on a road bike. We're well over 200bhp these days on our superstock bikes, which use treaded road tyres and superbikes on slicks aren't making that much more power, so we're pretty much limited by how much grip the rear tyre has. The point is that there's actually nothing new about needing one or maybe even two specialists in the garage who can make the difference with the bikes' potential and increase the chances of the rider winning; today the specialist is an electronics expert; back then, especially when the bikes had two-stroke engines, it was an engine tuner.

You also need a bit of luck for your path to cross with that person who helps the rider get that extra 5% from the bike, and in Dad's case that was a fella called Fred Hagley. Fred owns and still works at Omega Pistons in Dudley, so calling in to see him and have a look around his factory has always been easy. In more recent times, Fred has made every piston used by the Ducati factory in all their V-twin factory superbike race bikes without a single failure – that's fourteen world championships and seven British championships. He also made every piston used in Ducati's MotoGP engines for a ten-year period, including the world title with Casey Stoner in 2007. Other notable racing Ducatis which had Fred's pistons in include the one that Mike Hailwood used for his comeback at the Isle of Man TT in 1978, one of the greatest fairy-tale stories in the history of motorcycle racing. There is also the Judd, Renault, Ferrari and Cosworth Formula 1 engines that he made the pistons for until the mid-nineties, so he knows his stuff. Fred is in his eighties now and still opens up the factory for his eighteen staff to go about their day's work, but before Fred's rise in status and credibility in the world of engine design and tuning, there was Dad and Barry Randle, whose engines Fred worked on.

In the mid-sixties, Fred designed four motorcycle engines in his spare time while working at a local gunsmith: one for racing, one for karting, one for motocross, and one for his own 125cc bike, so even by the standards back then, he wasn't messing about when it came to how to fill your spare time.

The editor of a motorcycle magazine who knew Barry Randle asked Fred to go and look at Barry and his bikes to see if he could help. The editor said to Fred that Barry had a mate who when it comes to racing he hated, because he couldn't beat him as his bikes weren't quick enough. The mate that the editor was referring to was Dad. Fred had never tuned a Yamaha but went anyway to look at Barry's, and he took the top off the engine to have a look at the cylinder. He said to Barry that he thought he knew what to do, but he was worried about doing any work on the cylinders because they were plated with Nikasil, which, if damaged, could come away from the bore of the cylinder when the bike got started up and wreck the motor. Barry said he didn't care and to just do it because he was at Castle Coombe the following weekend, which is a fast track, and so expected Dad to wipe the floor with him. For Dad to be 350cc British champion, Fred explained, he had to win the race, plus his main rival Derek Chatterton had to finish in third place or lower.

Fred spent every night that week working on Barry's engines and took them to Castle Coombe without starting them up. Barry won the 250cc race, broke the lap record, and more importantly beat Dad by miles, but the 350cc race was the one that really mattered to Dad. Barry was leading it comfortably, enjoying his newfound power, while Dad was second and Derek was third, so at that point Dad was losing the championship. Then Barry went down the start/finish straight while fiddling with the clutch lever and let Dad come past, then he held off Derek so Dad became champion. That was in 1971 and it was his first British championship. He also became British champion again in 1973 when he won the 250cc title.

It must have been hard for Barry to do that, and Fred reckons that he regretted doing it until the day he died. He really hated Dad on the track, even though they were mates off it, but he obviously decided in the moment to help Dad out, otherwise he would have won both races. Why Barry chose to do it we'll never know, and I hope Dad thanked him – something he was notoriously not very good at doing.

Dave Burr, who was one of Dad's big sponsors towards the end of his career and who played a big part in supporting me and Mum while Dad recovered from his Montjuic Park injuries, told me that that he doesn't remember Dad ever saying 'thank you' to him, which pissed him off and hurt. I was disappointed but not surprised to hear this, so I gave Dave one of my TT trophies as a token of my appreciation for all that he did for Dad. I know it's not the same, and it doesn't really make up for the hurt, but I do believe that Dad was just so completely focused on racing that he simply didn't register stuff like that.

Dad had a mate called Fred Corbett, who used to give up his holidays and go to the TT to help him. He'd sleep in a caravan and work non-stop for the two and a half weeks that he was there, and Dave reckons he never heard Dad thank him or even say please, yet he somehow managed to get so much out of people. I think maybe it was a sign of the times, especially in those circles, that the chance to travel about a bit and be around bikes was very appealing, meaning that getting people to help and do things for you would have been quite easy for someone like Dad, I imagine.

Fred tuned the engines for Barry's race at Monza – the one Bob and Keith told me about. He raced a 350cc Yamaha TR2 against Jarno Saarinen, who was racing the factory Yamaha, and Giacomo Agostini, who should need no introduction and was there on his MV Agusta. Barry qualified third on the grid and got away with Agostini and Saarinen, but the Yamahas just couldn't touch the MV on Monza's long straights. However, every time they came to the main straight, Barry would pass Saarinen on the factory Yamaha, which Fred took a lot of pride in telling me. It also meant that Barry would have been able to out-drag Saarinen to the finish line for second place. Eventually a carb rubber on Barry's bike split, and he lost power so finished third. Nobody had ever heard of Barry before that, but when he went to the Race of the Year at Mallory Park a few months later, everyone knew him. Nothing changes there; it's the same today in the race paddock, where one day you're nobody, then you get a result and everyone wants to be your friend, then when the results dry up, everyone disappears.

Of course, Dad worked out that Barry's bikes had suddenly become faster than his due to Fred's input, so he started hassling Fred to tune his engines. To start with, Fred just prepared the crankshaft and repaired them when they needed rebuilding, until eventually Dad must have twisted his arm hard enough and Fred tuned an engine for Dad. Of course, when Barry found out, he was livid and fell out in a big way with Fred in the pub. It's something that happens all too often in racing, but that's the nature of the competition at a high level: people expect more of everything, including loyalty, which is a rare thing in the race paddock. It sounds like the break-up of Fred and Barry was pretty ugly, which, while unpleasant at the time, in my experience does make it easier in the end. Fred worked for Dad until the day he stopped racing Yamahas, which would have been around the late seventies.

As mentioned before, luckily Dad's big sponsor at the time, Bob Priest, had a haulage firm, and Fred only lived about 300 yards from the garage, which also happened to be next door to the pub. So, Fred and Dad used to go to the pub all the time back then, which Fred reckons is probably why he got divorced. He was either working on his bikes at Bob Priest's garage or in the pub next door, plus Fred went to every race with Dad, which is where he and a bloke called Professor Gordon Blair would compare notes. Blair was the head of research at Queens University Belfast (QUB) and looked up Fred at the North West 200 because Dad's bikes were so fast. I think there was a lot of mutual respect between them as engineers because Fred, who is one of the cleverest people I know, describes Blair as 'a very clever man,' which is high praise. As well as being clever, Blair must also have been very persuasive because eventually Fred made some parts for him.

Queens University Belfast's long association with bike racing was originally established in the mid-sixties by Blair, who was then already a professor of mechanical engineering. He decided to combine his passion for motorbikes with his position in the university to set about a process of researching, designing and building engines that they then entered into races in the Irish road race scene as a way of proving them. He and his department at the university were some of the early pioneers in the late sixties to have figured out how to use computer simulation to figure out optimum engine designs. They became such a technical force that in the early 1970s Yamaha approached the university and entered a technical agreement with them to help them with their engine designs for many years. Eventually Blair became the Dean of Engineering at the university, so he had to step back from the day-to-day research, but the university carried on making fast two-stroke race engines pretty much right up until they got phased out of racing. Notably, they were heavily involved with Jeremy McWilliams in the late nineties, when he was racing competitively in the 250cc Grand Prix championship

In the mid to late '70s Ray McCullough was the QUB rider, and Ray was a big name in the Irish road race scene. He was noted as one of the very few people who could beat Joey Dunlop at the time, but he couldn't beat Dad at the North West 200 in 1977. Famously, the two of them were credited with a dead-heat finish in the 350cc race, which to this day remains as the only dead heat at the North West 200, and to my knowledge any motorcycle race. Fred was there for the dead heat in '77 and was in the pits for the race, which is one of the few places you can see the start/finish line. Fred thought Dad won it and remembers him coming up to Ray from behind as they approached the start/finish line and getting alongside him as they crossed the line; the atmosphere must have been amazing. Fred says he was looking at it sort of head on, and obviously Dad also thought he won, and Ray thought he won too, but if you look at the photo it's a dead heat. Dad's engine had been tuned by Fred, and Ray's had been tuned by QUB, so it was a dead heat between Fred and Gordon Blair too.

A few years before the dead heat, probably 1973 or 1974, Fred tuned Dad's four-cylinder Yamaha TZ750cc engine by adding an extra port in the back for the reed valve, and at the Northwest 200 it did 186mph down the straight and coming back the other way, with the wind behind it, it did over 190mph. However, because they only time the bikes on the first long straight there, he was credited with 186mph, which is mind-blowing, and at the North West 200 being able to do those sorts of speeds is a massive help. These days, if your bike can't do 200mph there, you'll be nowhere. It doesn't sound like a lot more than Dad was doing in the 1970s, but there are chicanes and all sorts now to deliberately slow us down, so it's not really comparable. Nonetheless, the thought of sitting on one of those things, with the brakes and tyres and suspension they had at the time, and doing 190mph is terrifying, and that's before you consider the added element of the danger of the engine seizing, which a lot of them did in those days. Fair play to them all.

Fred remembers Dad getting hold of an Offenstadt chassis, which by all accounts back then was revolutionary. The chassis itself was a monocoque design, which was very forward-thinking at the time, and it also had a single shock absorber at the rear. Nowadays a single shock absorber set up is not just common, it's the standard set-up for pretty much all motorcycles. Back then it was like witchcraft, and the Offenstadt was one of the first – if not the first – motorcycle chassis to use a mono-shock set-up. Dad and Fred were at the side of a track somewhere watching a race when someone went past on an Offenstadt, and they both looked at each other and said, 'Bloody hell, look at the suspension on that.' It made the track look much smoother than it was; the bike was so much more settled and stable than everything else out there. They were both taken by how well it seemed to handle.

Predictably, Dad said he wanted one, so he went to see Bob Priest, and an Offenstadt chassis was found, with no engine. When it turned up, Fred thought it was a bag of nails, so he got to work on it. They got it sorted and Fred fitted a tuned-up 350cc engine in it. It's hard to know what that engine would have made back then. This would have been 1975, and today a tuned 250cc two-stroke engine can produce 100bhp, but in Dad's day his 250cc race bike would have made about 45bhp, which would have been considered very good. Today a 125cc two-stroke engine will make over 50bhp, which makes you realise engine development has come such a long way. Fred also paid tribute to Dad's mechanic at the time, Colin. He said that he was brilliant and that Dad had a knack for finding really good mechanics. I think he knew the value of them, plus there's the small matter that Dad could only do so much with the spanners. He would always say that if his engine seized he would be able to 'catch it', which is to say that he could feel it just starting to seize and pull the clutch in before the engine actually seized and locked the gearbox, in turn locking the rear wheel and more than likely throwing him over the handle-bars. It's milliseconds between the engine starting to seize and actually seizing, and if you're alert to it and have a feeling for it, you can sometimes 'catch it', but Fred reckons Dad never did!

When Bob Priest died it was a really big deal. He was a popular guy in the area and obviously a very big part of Dad's early success. Luckily, a fella called Sid Griffiths, who owned a car dealership in Lye, took over sponsoring Dad until 1981, which was the point when Dad first got involved with Ducatis and Steve Wynne at Sports Motorcycles. Around the same time, Fred's business was really starting to take off, so it suited him that Dad's career was heading on to four-stroke bikes. It meant that Fred could pull back from tuning Dad's two-stroke Yamaha engines and focus on his business – although he did still make the pistons for Dad's Ducatis, and he also tuned the engine in Dad's Suzuki RG500 that he raced in the Senior TT in 1979. The Bob Priest and

Fred Hagley era of Dad's career was a great spell for both Bob and Fred as they were each making a mark for themselves in their respective fields, and in the end it ran its natural course.

During the next few years on Ducatis, Dad teamed up with a mechanic called Pat Slinn; he was a fantastic mechanic and played a big part in a lot of Dad's TT wins and his world championships. Years later something went wrong between Pat and Dave Burr, which I always kept out of. Then, in 2008, when we had built one of Dad's Ducatis for him to do a parade lap at the TT, Pat appeared and started saying that it wasn't Dad's Ducati and making a bit of a scene. The thing is, pretty much any old race bike has been messed about with, and they're very rarely exactly as they came off the track when they last raced. Everyone knows that Dad's bike got snapped in two at Montjuic Park, so for the parade lap we got parts from his bikes from that year and made one. Pat was very bitter, and I don't really understand why because if Dad was still here, and had to build one again, that's how he would build it. Then, he had all the parts for it at his house for ten years, just tinkering with them, so using them to make the bike seemed obvious. The only bike I can say is identical to when it finished the race is my Honda RCV213V, and the race in question was the 2019 Macau GP, which I won. The reason the RCV is identical to how it crossed the line is that I can't afford the expensive parts that it needs for a refresh!

Fred, who reckons he can always spot a good rider, said that nobody knew why Dad was so good. If you look at Hailwood, the greatest bike racer at the time, probably ever, he certainly never moved his bum one way or the other but just sat in the middle of the bike and obliterated everyone. It doesn't make any sense how some riders just make it look easy. Fred reckons that Paul Smart and John Cooper started the hanging-off riding style in the UK – a technique that makes it a lot easier to spot how hard someone is trying. It's a fine line between being average and brilliant; the last 5% is the hardest, and it usually comes when you're in a good mood and relaxed. It's a state of mind.

Just like Dad, I've gone through my career and worked with some incredible mechanics, engine tuners and more recently electronic engineers. I've ridden for full-factory teams like HRC, and I've ridden for teams with huge budgets, and in 2009, when I found myself out of a ride just before the TT, I got a few mates together and went racing out the back of a van again. As Fred says, the difference a good crew can make to a rider's state of mind is massive. I am a piss-taker and I wind people up, but I also like to have the piss taken out of me.

The Penz13 team that I rode for in 2015 was a German team, so when we went testing I obviously got stuck into them, taking the piss out of them because they didn't win the war. After the test finished, we went out for dinner, and Marcus Reitenberger was there – he is a really nice lad and so unbelievably quick on the bike. Everyone was having a great time, and the war banter started up again, but I might have been a bit pissed because I evidently took it a bit too far and went on about the Spitfires and how we were just better at everything. They all thought it was really funny at first, but when I started really breaking it down on how we won and going on about it, they didn't seem so amused. Eventually one of them got really angry with me. You know when you sober up the next day and you think what a dickhead you are? That was me. At the time I was forty-three years old and should have known better, but it's one of many examples of me not being able to read the room very well. I never got to say sorry because I never saw him again. He didn't come to any of the races, so the atmosphere was great in that team despite me doing my best to ruin it, and we had a really good season and a lot of fun that year.

But it's not just getting on with the people in your garage that makes a difference –it's brilliant when the atmosphere in the whole paddock is great. I've said it before, and anyone who's raced on both short circuits and the roads will agree: the atmosphere and piss-taking between everyone in the road race paddock is much better. After the Macau GP every year all the teams would go to Thailand for a holiday as part of the deal for going to Macau to race. Every year, the same people would go to the same hotel, the same beach, the same bar and after a few years all the staff knew us by our first names. There was a mechanic who used to work for MSS Kawasaki called Tricky, and one year for some reason he didn't come to the beach with us. All the staff were asking where he was, so we decided to take the piss: we told them that he was dead. They couldn't believe it and were being really sombre and respectful to us; they were gutted and went round just telling people, 'Tricky dead.' Later in the day, Tricky appeared and sat down with us. All the staff were shocked to see him and realised that we were taking the piss, so they spent the night going along with the joke, proclaiming 'Tricky alive!' The following year when we went to Thailand, Tricky had, in fact, died some time before the Macau GP, so obviously he wasn't there, and when we told the staff that he had died, they didn't believe us and kept going 'Tricky alive', expecting him to appear. No matter how many times we told them that this time he was actually dead, they didn't believe us.

It's amazing the number of people you come into contact with during a career as a bike racer, and the higher the level you compete at, the more people you need, plus nowadays the amount of staff that some teams have is eye-watering, but the same fundamental truth applies: every great racer, whatever the era, needs other people to get to the top.

4
We Aren't Normal

I think I talked a bit about how us racers are wired differently to most people and how we just don't see the danger in things or how we are unbelievably selfish, and especially how we are so competitive that even the most stupid things become matters of life and death and where everything is a competition. I see it in my daughters, Juliette and Cecillia. They are really competitive, maybe Cecillia is a bit more than Juliette, but I couldn't believe how Juliette was in a go-kart – you can see it in her eyes; she's so determined. Neither of them will give an inch. Even a family game of table tennis gets angry and we will fall out, and it just gets worse because as soon as someone gets in a sulk, it's game on and we'll take the mickey out of them to really ram home the point that they lost. Even the piss-taking is competitive, and I do think it's nice to see that in them, but thank God I've got two girls because I reckon if they were boys, it would end up in proper fist-fights. Neither of them took up a sport competitively, and I often wonder why, considering how competitive they are.

I never did any stuff like go-karting or table tennis with Dad; he'd only do stuff with me if he was interested in it himself. When I was a bit older I wanted to go model car racing and I remember going to Kidderminster, and Dad said he'd take me and drop me off, and he would pick me up later but only if I really needed him to, but I should try and get a lift back with someone else. At the end of the day I couldn't get a lift home with anyone, so I ended up walking two hours back home from Kidderminster. It was normal for Dad to just forget like that. I know they were different times, and I'm sure when I was at the peak of my career I could have done more things with my kids, but I do have a lot more memories of doing stuff with them that I suspect Dad did of doing stuff with me.

When the kids used to ask me for money, I'd say that it doesn't grow on trees, and they, Cecillia especially, would say that it does, just to wind me up. As I'm always trying to get the last word, I thought I'd teach them a lesson and said to them to go and check the tree at the end of the driveway for some money. They said, 'Yeah OK, whatever', because we were going out anyway, so they went along with it and had a look. I'd been out earlier and paper-clipped some money to the tree, and when the girls saw it they were shaking their heads and laughing at me, thinking only I could do that. Imagine if someone else walked past and saw the money!

When Mum had just gone into hospital, Juliette, Cecillia and I had been to visit her, and we arrived home and pulled up at the gates to my house. They're automatic, but when I pressed the button to open them, nothing happened. You can unlock them manually with a safety key if they don't open, but the key was in the house, so I had to climb over the gate. The problem with that plan was that they hadn't been working the day before either, and there must have been an electrical cable that had shorted out because when I grabbed hold of the gate to climb over it there was a flash of power that electrocuted me and lit me up in the dark, much to my daughters' alarm. It also shorted the whole house, just to finish off a shitty day. So, the next day when I got back from the hospital with the kids we got to the gate and it wasn't working again, so I said to Juliette to just jump over the gate (as it wasn't very high) and fetch the key, but she'd seen what happened the day before and said she wouldn't do it, so I said, 'Bloody hell, I'll show you.' I ran up to the gate put my foot on one of those sharp spear-shaped things, that are part of it's design and it went straight through my trainer and into my foot. Now I was limping and trying to run up the drive with blood all over the place, and the kids just laughed at me. I couldn't really be angry because if it was the other way round, I probably would have laughed at them too.

It reminded me of when I lived with Mum and Dad at Crestwood Park. I had been out on my Suzuki TS50X moped. As I was coming home, I saw Dad was at the letter box at the end of our street, and on the approach to it there was a sharp double-apex corner a bit like the hairpin at Mallory Park. I came round the corner trying to impress Dad, hit a drain cover and nearly crashed. The rear of the bike slid round into a massive highside, but somehow I stayed on it. When I pulled up at home, Dad came up to me and just said, 'You are a bloody dickhead', and that was all I got! He wasn't very hands-on, Dad.

I also remember going with Dad to the Isle of Man in his transit van when I was about nine or ten years old. It's funny the things you remember: the ferry was called the Lady of Mann and it had rickety wooden boarding ramps. Dad hid me in the footwell to avoid spending a fiver or whatever it was for my ticket. I would go down to the bottom of the ship because there was a cinema room there, and when the sea was rough everyone would just be puking all over the place; it was terrible, just plodding along really slowly surrounded by people throwing up. When we docked, Dad would tell me to just walk up the vehicle ramp, not the passenger one, and without giving it a second thought, I'd just get out of Dad's van and sneak off the boat, dodging all the officials, and then meet up with him in the docks, jump back into his van and carry on like it was the most normal thing. He was just a typical bike racer, always trying to get away with not paying for something. I think it held an irresistible thrill for him.

Dad used to have some mad ideas, a bit like I do sometimes. When the law changed and everyone had to wear seatbelts in the car, he just would not wear one, so he got this idea of putting some black vinyl across his shoulder so it looked like he had his seatbelt on. It was so stupid, not just because of the obvious risk to his safety and the fact he was breaking the law, but because he went to so much effort to make the vinyl look like a seatbelt and it would have been easier to just put the belt on. But that was his way; he was always just trying to get away with not conforming, which I think is a characteristic of a lot of racers. We defy the majority, even common sense at times; us racers treat everything as a competition. There is literally nothing we can't make competitive.

Dave Heal was the British Supersport champion with V&M Racing, and he was so competitive. He was a really nice lad but so competitive that it was really annoying, even for me. He had to be the best at everything. He was a very popular guy that got on with everyone and could have the piss taken out of him no problem. We were testing with the V&M team at San Marino, so it was me, Ian Simpson and Dave all together, with me and Ian on Honda RC45s and Dave on his 600, so I guess it would have been 1997. We were staying in a hotel, and Dave used to smoke cigarettes a lot, so we used to hide them and wind him up by saying it was probably the cleaner who took them, knowing full well that he'd march over to reception and kick off. Anyway, we were in a pub and Ian says, 'Come on, then, Dave. If you think you're fit, let's have a competition'. The competition was that we all sat up against this wall and you had to hold yourself up and see who lasted the longest. So, there we all were, squatting with our backs against a wall, holding ourselves up in basically what amounts to a torture position. I thought, sod this, I'd rather drink, so I went and sat back down with the rest of the team while Dave and Simmo carried on. They were clearly in agony, with sweat dripping off them, but even though it was a daft alcohol-fuelled pub game, it became almost a matter of life and death for both of them. Neither wanted to back down no matter how much pain they were in, until eventually Dave collapsed, meaning Simmo won. It's just the nature of the beast; we've all got that streak, just some have it more than others. I was told a story once about how apparently Troy Bayliss had smashed the brake light lens on his paddock scooter with his bare fist for a bet the night before a race. He then spent the rest of the night picking bits of lens plastic out of the back of his hand, just because he couldn't back down and say no. I don't think Dad would have got involved in that sort of stuff; in a lot of ways we were very similar in so much as for us it only mattered on the track.

It's not just the extreme competitive streak that we racers share; we've also got quite a dark sense of humour and don't always react in the same way that normal people do. It was at Dad's funeral that I was reminded of this by one of Dad's very good friends, Mick Windsor. Mick was a local gardener and used to take care of Dad's parents' garden – my grandparents'. He got to know Dad that way when they were young, and even though Mick was also a very skilled race mechanic I don't think he ever worked as Dad's mechanic. He told me a story about when he and one of Dad's mechanics called Fred (a different one) went to my nan's funeral – that's Dad's mum.

Mick and Fred went to the funeral in Fred's van and parked round the back of the church. When the service was over, everyone was milling around outside before heading over to the crematorium next. The pair went around the back of the church, got in the van and drove to Stourbridge crematorium. When they got there, there were blokes in overalls decorating the place, and no sign of a funeral. They asked what was going on, only to be told that the crematorium was closed for redecorating, and they had to go to Gornall, about six miles away. Nobody had told them to go to Gornall crematorium. Mick and Fred decided there wasn't enough time, and that they would miss it, so they decided to just drive back to Mum and Dad's house for the wake. When they got there, who should meet them on the doorstep but Dad! When Mick and Fred asked him what he was doing there and not at the crematorium, he answered, 'I'm not bloody going up there. She's alright on her own. They'll sort her out. C'mon in and have a cup of tea.' It just typified the bloke. Racing was all he ever lived for; it was all that mattered to him.

Mick told me that Dad just left him on the ferry back from Northern Ireland once after the North West 200 one year. The story goes that Mick's rider was staying on in Ireland to attend to business (apparently she was really nice), so Mick arranged a lift back to the Midlands with Dad. When they got on the boat, Dad had more than his usual half shandy and, along with everyone else, got really drunk. Eventually everyone decided it was time to get some sleep, and everything was fine for Mick until the morning after, when he woke up and realised that they had been docked for three hours. He got out of bed and off the boat and everyone had gone; Dad had just left him. Poor old Mick had to get all sorts of trains, buses and taxis until he eventually got to Mum and Dad's house, only to be told by Mum that Dad was down the pub. When Mick got to the pub there was another party happening, with Dad telling everyone about his week's racing. Then when he saw Mick, who was the best part of a day behind Dad getting home, he just said in his broad Black Country accent, ''Ere he is, wers yow bin?', and when Mick told him his story about how he had to get off the boat and get back home on his own, all Dad did was laugh and laugh at Mick's bad day. Mick did manage to ask Dad why he left him on the ship and, still laughing at him, all Dad said was that he couldn't see him, but it was more like he just plain forgot about the fact he'd agreed to give Mick a lift home. Mick says that he managed to involve most of the pub with the story, and somehow, even though the joke was on Mick, he says it was actually a nice end to the week because Dad's laugh was really infectious, and his shoulders would dance up and down.

Something I already knew about Dad, and can also see in myself, was just how laid back he was. One year at the TT during Thursday afternoon practice, the riders used to go out on all different machinery in one session, which is something we still do today. Dad had been out on his 750 Yamaha for a lap, then swapped onto his 350cc for a lap. Mick happened to be standing watching from a spot just down from the Gooseneck. He saw what he thought was Dad's bike going careering through a gateway and into a field, so he went down the road for a better look but couldn't see and couldn't get across to do anything for him. There were people there and Dad was OK, just knocked about a bit. A few weeks later Mick went into Dad's shop to see how he was, and to tell him that he'd seen the crash and wondered what had happened. Apparently, Dad said that he'd been out on the 750, and his 350 felt really slow, and he thought he just switched off and fell asleep. He said he recalled coming to his senses, but it was too late and luckily there was a gate that he could hit and go through instead of hitting the brick wall, so he got off lightly. He never even tried to make the corner, so he must have been daydreaming right up to when he went through the gate.

At least he was honest. A lot of riders would have bullshitted and never admitted to simply not concentrating enough, but he was so lucky the gate was there. Dad did tell me the same story once and said that he was thinking of the 750 that he'd been riding on the previous lap, which wasn't right. He told me that the 350 was so good that he was riding around on it thinking about how to make the 750 better, so he wasn't really daydreaming as such; he was at least thinking about something, just not what he was supposed to be focusing on. I've had the same thing happen to me during practice after swapping bikes mid-session. I've caught myself thinking, 'Fucking hell, I've got to get back on that thing when I get back and the end of this lap', and in the time it takes to have that thought on the TT course, you can be in a whole world of trouble.

A racer's relationship with risk and danger is something else that sets us apart; we either don't see it at all or, if we do, it doesn't seem as risky as it actually is. I believe that's what's at the heart of why we're able to go fast – that and the competitive streak which we also have. Not having an active imagination means that we don't think to ourselves, 'What if?', so the thought about what might happen to us if something goes wrong on the bike never enters our heads until it has actually gone wrong. It's not just on the bike though; Dad told me that one time when he was racing at the Ulster Grand Prix, he was staying at a house in Belfast. The lady who owned it told Dad that things were a bit dodgy at the time, and he shouldn't really go out, but Dad said, 'I do what I bloody want' and went out for a walk. He told me that soon after he set off, a bullet hit the floor near him and ricocheted off the wall next to him. He says it was at that moment he thought he should probably get back to the house. I don't know if it's true but that's what he told me and, knowing him as I did, I wouldn't be surprised if it was true because if someone ever said to him that he couldn't do something, he'd make a point of doing it.

I checked the story with Mick, and he said that sort of thing was happening at the time in Northern Ireland, so it's quite possible that the story is true. Looking back, Mick says, the Troubles didn't seem to bother them because they always felt so welcome everywhere they went. Even though they were in the heart of it, the Troubles were something that they saw on the news rather than first-hand. Mick and Dad used to go up the Falls Road on purpose to take a look, and Dad used to say that he would take the people from Ducati there because all they wanted to do was drive up and down the Falls Road, so he would put them in his van and drive up and down it with them. They were fascinated by the burnt-out cars and soldiers with guns; he said to me that the Italians were more interested in the Falls Road than the racing.

At the Classic TT one year, I was racing a Matchless G50, just trying to get it to the end of the race. When you race you just want to finish and you want to win, even though there are warning signs all over the place that you should probably stop or at least back off. The bike was vibrating so badly that I literally couldn't feel my hands. Through the race it got worse and worse and by the final lap I wasn't sure I could hold on – plus by then my eyesight had also gone and my feet were numb too. Stupidly I never thought that the bike could also be about to fall apart. You'd think that given how much the bike was hurting me I would have wondered whether the bike was about to fall apart, but it never entered my mind. Eventually, as I was tipping into Greeba Bridge, which is a fast left-hander in about third gear on the classic bike, it locked up and went sideways, skidding to a halt. Without question, if it had happened 5 seconds earlier, I'd have crashed. The rear wheel nut had unwound itself, and even though it was lock-wired to the bike, it had moved enough to loosen the rear wheel. It had even shaken so much that it wound off the caps that hold the front wheel on; it was literally shaking itself apart, but you're so focused on finishing that you just can't see the warning signs.

Mick and Dad were really good mates right to the end, and Mick used to take care of Mum and Dad's garden too, just like he had my grandparents'. I think he did it mostly so he could go and visit Dad when he started to get sick, without making it obvious. I also think that the odd jobs around the house that Dad found for Mick were things he could have probably done for himself, but I think Dad just wanted to keep some sort of contact with his racing past. Mick basically confirmed it to me when he came round for a coffee soon after Dad's funeral. He told me that giving up racing was probably one of the most difficult things for Dad simply because he was 110% racing for his whole life and couldn't diversify when he had to stop. He would call Mick to say his car wouldn't start, but really he wanted someone else to talk to about racing and to try and recreate the racing family and atmosphere.

Dad was miserable and lost his motivation and interest in anything once he got ill. As soon as Dad got ill, he was doomed. A prime example of someone finding a new life after racing is Roger Marshall; he's never left the paddock, filling various roles to do with rider safety and representation in British Superbikes, and he has recently taken on a new role at Yamaha to do with rider coaching, a bit like he did with the Medd Kawasaki team in my first year as a pro. He's the same as Dad in so much as I think he never left racing, but unlike Dad, Roger found a way to stay involved. Some riders find a new purpose in racing, and others find it extremely difficult, and Dad definitely did struggle. The problem is that racing has a lot of glamour, a lot of excitement, thrill and danger – it's a big hole to fill.

Mick used to get so infuriated with Dad because he was offered help when he was ill, and I believe if he took it, he might even still be here. He certainly would have had a happier retirement, but he never took it. He did everything on his terms, and if you didn't fit in with him, he didn't have anything to do with you; that attitude was powerful and without doubt a big part of why he achieved so much in racing, but it really didn't help him in later in life. Mick reckons he'll go down as extremely well recognised and respected in the racing fraternity, but he doesn't think Dad ever got recognised enough for his world championships.

It does take a certain breed, and it does take something to be prepared to do whatever it takes to beat the person who's also your friend. Mick said that Dad had that characteristic in spades, but he doesn't see it in me, that I always have a degree of safety on my mind, which is both a strength and a weakness. There are riders whose only focus in life is to be champion, and they will smash themselves and others who get in the way to pieces in order to do that, but they will achieve their goal. Then there are riders who want to earn a long-term living out of it and treat it as a career and who have managed to do it with a lot of success along the way. The ones who only want to win and leave when they do because they achieved their goal then find themselves wondering 'What next?' They won't make much money out of being a racer. Tommy Hill springs to mind; he won the British Superbike championship in 2011 and retired straight away. It was as though he did what he came to do, and now he has a whole new life as a graphic designer. Hats off to him, but my approach has always been different, I want to race forever, and Dad wanted to race forever; the difference is that I don't know if he ever worked out that he couldn't do that from a hospital bed. He also would have raced for nothing, which is always going to limit how long you can do it for.

People get different things out of racing. We're all out there racing each other, and we all want to win and beat each other, yet we're all there on different journeys that aren't always clear at the time. I never thought I'd still be racing and able to earn a living out of it at the age of fifty, but the fact that I am means I've somehow made a proper career out of it, even though I've never won the British championship. Dad won two British championships, four world championships and eight TTs but was very bitter and lonely when his racing ended. In contrast at the other end of the scale I read or saw somewhere that Guy Martin has made more money than any racer ever has since he stopped racing, but that all started with his ability to ride a bike. I bet any money when he started out with a head full of dreams of being a champion and winning TT races, he never thought he'd achieve neither one, yet end up as a global superstar and very well off because of the doors that bike racing opened for him.

In *The Life of a Racer* I mentioned that Dad taught me a lot about racing without realising it. There's no question that I inherited a lot of his traits, which to be fair are common in pretty much every racer that makes it to a high standard. We're selfish, competitive, don't see danger where others do. A lot of that stuff is in my genes, but Dad also taught me stuff by me recognising his mistakes and not repeating them.

5
Endurance

One form of racing that I've never liked much is endurance racing, but when you're a professional racer, and especially if you're riding for a manufacturer, it's just one of those things that you have to do. Over the years, I've raced in all the big endurance races and there's no denying that the Bol d'Or, Le Mans and Suzuka 8 Hours are all really big deals to the factories, and the crowds that go to the races are massive. As it turns out, through a chat with Roger Marshall I discovered that Dad also hated doing them which I never knew, but could probably have guessed. Roger really shouldn't need any introduction, but in the seventies and eighties he was the man to beat in the British championship. He won eleven championships, and just like Dad he won at the North West 200 and Ulster Grand Prix, but he never quite managed a TT win, or the F1 world championship, in which he finished second a few times.

A much more impressive achievement than all of that, though, is that Roger did all the riding for David Essex as his stunt double in the film *Silver Dream Racer,* which is one of the greatest films of all time. I don't know if it was wishful thinking on my part or my imagination getting carried away, but I always had it in my head that Dad was somehow involved in the making of that film, but sadly, while he thinks Dad may have been one of the backup riders, Roger can't remember if he was in the film. However, one thing he was certain of is that David Essex was only insured to ride the motorbikes up to 15mph during filming, which resulted in a problem: there couldn't be any smoke coming from the exhausts, of the bike but a two-stroke engine at low speeds would produce plenty. So, Roger would have to ride round the track at full speed to clear any smoke, pull up to a mark, jump off the bike and David Essex would get on it and ride off at 15mph smoke-free. The filmmakers split the shot to make it look like he'd just pulled up on it. David Essex said that he did all the riding in the film which, Roger took a lot of pleasure telling me, is a load of bollocks.

Even though Dad's career took off some years before Roger's did, their careers did overlap for a long time, and while he and Dad were competitors for most of that time, they were briefly team-mates in the World Endurance Championship. It's a part of Dad's career that I really didn't know much about, and Roger was kind enough to share some of his memories of his time with Dad.

Roger told me that he had been following racing since he was seven years old when his dad took him to Cadwell Park. In the sixties Roger was still dreaming about being a rider and Dad was one of the people that he had come to really admire in the 350cc and 250cc classes. I suppose when you think of the pedigree of the people he was racing against then – people like Charlie Williams, John Williams, Graham McGregor, Steve Machin and Mick Grant, and bear in mind a lot of the times Dad was coming out on top on his way to winning his British championships – I suppose it's understandable to see why Dad should be looked up to by anyone wanting to get into racing.

When Roger eventually started racing, he did sidecar racing, so his path didn't cross with Dad's until he started racing solos at national level. Apparently, it was at a race at Croft in 1974, when I was two years old, that Roger and Dad had their first conversation. It was the who's who of the British championship at the time, all in the 350cc race, and Croft was one of the tracks that Roger cut his teeth on, so he went well there. He reckons he didn't know that there was prize money up for grabs and that obviously Dad did, which is possible because I know what it's like when you're starting out – all you want to do is get involved, beat the established riders and make your mark. Everybody who had been a British champion or a runner-up was on that grid, and Roger was just having one of those days and kept passing everyone until with about two laps to go he was up to second position behind Dad. He followed Dad to the chequered flag and was just happy to be on the podium with him, which is where they had their first conversation. Despite Roger saying it was one of the best rides he ever had and being chuffed to share the podium with Dad, he soon regretted not having a go at passing him after someone pointed out that there was prize money and that it was £1,000 to win the race and £550 quid for second place! Even so, it was the most money he'd ever won; enough to buy a car.

The next time Roger's and Dad's paths crossed was a few years later, in 1975, when Dad was racing 750s. Dad was riding for Honda in world endurance and his original teammate got injured, so Honda approached Roger and he stepped in, with the blessing of his sponsor. Roger's first-ever endurance race was with Dad at Spa-Francorchamps on the old circuit, and it was a baptism of fire for him. It was a twenty-four-hour race, and back then there were just two riders per bike, and each session on track lasted for two hours each. Nowadays there are three riders per bike, even for the eight-hour race at Suzuka, and in fact before the race there are often more than the three riders who start the race meeting.

In 1999, Kawasaki France asked me to ride in the Bol d'Or at the Paul Ricard circuit, but I didn't realise that all through practice and qualifying it was a competition between me and Steve Plater for the chance to take part in the race; I thought we were all in the team. During the practice sessions, I went out a few times and I didn't really get on with the bike; the set-up was so weird, and I have to have things how I like them. Then, out of nowhere, they told me that Steve was quicker than me so they were going to use him in the race, and that I could go home. I couldn't believe it and told them that if I knew it was a competition between us, I'd have tried a bit harder. It was my fault, and you could argue that I should have been flat out in the practice sessions, but in endurance racing you have to be 100% fit for the race, and grid position isn't as critical as it is in a normal thirty-minute race, so spannering yourself in practice for a couple of extra places up the grid isn't wise. Anyway, they said to just wait around and if no one crashed in morning warm-up, I could go home and I'd still get paid, so I thought fair enough.

As soon as the race started, I thought I'd head for the ferry, so got in my motorhome and set off. I was driving out the track through the car park and campsite, through all the French fans, who were pissed. Some of them jumped onto the railing on the back of my motorhome, just hanging onto it and swinging off it. There were about three of them on the back of it and one was sitting on the back of my scooter, which was fastened to a rack on the back of the motorhome. I got rid of the other two by braking hard here and there, until there was one left, pretending to be clever, so I accelerated loads and went really fast, then slammed the brakes on so hard that the bloke flew off the scooter onto the back window of the motorhome, then into a heap on the floor in a cloud of dust. I drove away while he was still there on the floor, doing my best to spin up some more dust onto him.

From the sound of it, Roger was quite lucky in so much as he said that he and Dad liked the same set-up on the bike, which is a rare thing. Later on, Roger would be teammate to the likes of Wayne Gardner, Ron Haslam and Joey Dunlop in endurance racing, and in the case of Ron Haslam Roger really struggled because he just couldn't get on with Ron's set-up and would be up to 15 seconds off Ron's pace at some of the races with long laps, which I totally get. Trying to go really fast on someone else's set-up is so difficult unless you're one of those rare breeds of racers who would still be fast if you put the back wheel in the front and the front wheel in the back, like Karl Harris was. Roger reckoned Dad was really laid back and pretty much unflappable, and he really admired how Dad could ride anything fast, regardless of what it was. I guess there must be some truth in that because Dad was competitive on Nortons in the sixties, lightweight two-strokes in the seventies and four-stroke V-twins and inline four-cylinder engines in the eighties.

It was Roger's first endurance race, and he says it was a big shock to his system coming out of a caravan at 2 a.m. freezing cold, to make your way over to the pits and get ready for your next session on track. It's a strange feeling you get during that walk from motorhome to pit lane in the middle of the night; it feels a bit like you're in between worlds. You go from the peace and quiet of being in bed asleep to still being alone but with the familiar sights, sounds and smells of a race whilst building yourself up to what you've got to do for the next hour or so and trying to wake up and motivate yourself. Then, when you get to the garage, it might as well be the middle of the day: all your senses are awake and fully alert, and your mind is focused on the task just as if it were the moments before a race or qualifying session.

Roger was telling me that in that first endurance race with Dad they were dicing for the lead for the whole race, and when daylight broke he was chuffed to bits. It was about 6 a.m., but they still had to get to 4 p.m., so there was a fair bit of racing still to do, and Roger had got himself ready to do his next shift on the track and was in the garage waiting for dad to finish his shift. Unbeknown to everyone, Dad had broken down not too far from the pits, so he just walked straight back to the garage, and in front of all the top guys from Honda said, 'Don't worry, Roger. Go back to your caravan. It's shit itself.' The overriding memory of that moment for Roger wasn't the disappointment of not finishing the race, but that he'd never heard Dad swear until then. It was a typically understated and straight-to-the-point analysis, and that was the end of the race for them.

Honda chartered a plane for Roger and Dad the next day to get them back to Silverstone for a test. Roger reckons there was a massive storm going on, and it was only a small two-seater plane about the size of his garden shed. While he was pulling his hair out, terrified and stressed out during the flight, Dad just took it all in his stride and slept most of the way. They formed quite a nice friendship, which is a rare thing in the paddock, especially for Dad, who generally kept himself to himself. He always had his people close to him all the time and none of them were other racers, so it was lovely to hear Roger say that he felt he was lucky enough to be one of the people who did get to know Dad and get an insight into what he was about.

I understand that endurance racing is a great spectator sport; you can light a fire and relax with some mates and some beer and watch some bikes being raced, and the teams put so much into it to be at the top of their games. Dad used to say that when he was endurance racing, it was so hard that the European riders would have injections and all sorts to keep them going, and the English riders got nothing. The Europeans had the same sort of bikes as Dad and Roger did, but the French teams had everything, which is pretty much the way it still is these days. It's tough, and you're riding on the limit the whole time, and everyone used to get so excited about it, but I dreaded it. According to Roger, Dad said he hated it too and couldn't wait for the bike to blow up. To Honda it meant more to them than Grand Prix races did; they thought more of endurance racing than they did anything else, which in my mind is just mad. Apart from Dad, Roger is the only other person I've met who hated endurance racing as much as me and, like me, did it for the money or to try and climb the ladder a bit with a manufacturer.

To give you an idea of just how much it means to the likes of Honda, Roger told me a tale about the time he was at Le Mans when he was teamed up with Phil Read. Stan Woods and Charlie Williams were leading the championship on the other Honda, so they wanted Roger and Phil to get involved. There's a fast left-hander out the back of the circuit, and when Roger shut the throttle on the approach to it, it stuck open, and instead of slowing, the bike accelerated. He tried to hit the ignition kill switch, but it didn't shut the bike down, so it was still flat out when it should have been slowing down a bit. Somehow, he got onto the grass and into the gravel trap and he managed to keep it upright until it came to a stop, only to discover that it was on fire and flames were licking up under his crash helmet, burning his chin. He jumped off the bike and looked back to see that one of the valves from the engine's cylinder head had gone through the fuel tank, causing fuel to go all over the hot engine and ignite. He went back to the pits and the team were mad that he left the bike trackside, so made Roger go back and push it all the way back to the pits, which you can do in endurance racing, even though he told them it wasn't repairable. He had to go anyway, and when he eventually had pushed it all the way back, the mechanics in the garage were on their knees in floods of tears because the bike was destroyed.

In 1983, Dad raced at Daytona in Florida with his Ducati and finished the support Battle of the Twins race in third position, but he also took part in the much longer 200-mile Daytona 200 main event that basically had the who's who of Grand Prix racing in it. Kenny Roberts won it on his factory Yamaha, and Dad finished twenty-first, which doesn't sound great, but he was the first four-stroke finisher, beating Freddie Spencer, Ron Haslam and Doug Polen. Apparently, the prize money for finishing twenty-first in the 200 was significantly much more than for finishing third in the Battle of the Twins race.

However, the thing I remember the most about the race at Daytona was when Dad took a big swig of petrol from a bottle, thinking it was his drink. He was really sick after that and had to go to hospital, which meant I didn't get to go to Disney World after the race as planned. The next time I was at Daytona was when I was asked by the bloke that imported Buell into the UK if I wanted to go and test one there. They offered me a lot of money to do it, and I always liked the idea of going to another track that Dad raced at.

They brought this massive contract out that was like a phone book; you know, the Americans have to do it big. What with my dyslexia and stuff, I just opened a few pages of it and pretty much just said, 'Are you lot for real?' I'd never seen anything like it before … or since. The bloke just said to sign it at the back, so I did, but I still have no idea what I signed. After we'd done all the legal stuff, which all went right over my head, we went to meet Eric Buell, who owned the company and designed the bike. When he showed us the bike, it really didn't match the hype and build-up, with all the legal stuff we'd just been through, and I did my best to not look underwhelmed. I suppose it did look special in some ways, such as the brake disc was mounted on the outer rim of the front wheel instead of the inner hub, where they usually are mounted. Then he started it up and as it sat there ticking over, the whole bike was literally pushing itself upright off its side stand and falling back down, such was the amount of torque being generated by each power pulse.

We all went back to the hotel, and I was thinking I couldn't wait to ride the bike, mainly because I was going to get the chance to ride the Daytona circuit with its world-famous 31-degree banked corner. I'd never ridden a steeply banked corner, let alone the most famous of all, the one that Barry Sheene had his massive accident on in 1975. It's a beast of a corner taken absolutely flat out, which on some bikes is north of 170mph, so I was really revved up about taking it on.

That night, a massive tornado came to the region and Miami, which is about 300 miles away, got shut down, so all the ambulances had to be taken from Daytona back to Miami all week, meaning we couldn't test the bike. With no testing on the cards, we just spent the whole time drinking, and because they don't have proper beer, we were drinking these cocktails called Blue Lagoons. We just went round different places drinking on Daytona beach, looking out to sea, and you could see the storm with its lightning and clouds, yet it was so still where we were. Eventually the storm did hit us, but it was nothing like what Miami got; it was turning over cars and aeroplanes there, but just the sight of it miles away in the distance was spooky, like the end of the world while we were just sitting on the beach drinking cocktails. Fair play to Buell, they still paid me even though I never rode the bike and just went home a professional drinker.

For someone who didn't like endurance racing, Dad did a lot of it. In 1982 he took part in the famous Suzuka 8 Hours race with George Fogarty as his teammate. Mum and Dad took me with them for the trip, which was amazing, although the worst bit was when we got home: I had to stand up at school assembly and tell everyone about where I'd been. This race was another part of Dad's career that I really don't know a lot about, but I do know that George's son Carl wasn't there, so I had to go to the man himself and see what George could tell me about the trip.

They were in Japan for two weeks and spent a lot of time just wandering around Tokyo, which is when the story I told in *The Life of a Racer* about getting left behind on a Tokyo street by everyone, aged ten, happened. Dad and George were using George's F1 specification Ducati for the race, but George had crashed it at the TT, at the bottom of Bray Hill. The story I've heard is that George went off at the start, crashed and no one could find him until eventually he turned up in a pub, which George denies. His bike caught fire in the middle of the road so it was a mess and couldn't be repaired properly before it had to be shipped to Japan. Pat Slinn, who was Dad's mechanic at the time, was working on it for a week at the Ducati dealer in Tokyo to get it sorted, even getting help from Honda to straighten the forks. By the sound of it, Dad and George got treated like royalty when they were over there, getting taken out for functions and dinners with all sorts of people. It was a big team with another bike ridden by some Americans, and it was all paid for by a sponsor called Kenny. Nobody knew what he did or where his money came from, but he had plenty of it and wasn't afraid to spend it.

Going by what George told me, he and Dad were a right pair of Brits on tour in Tokyo. They'd just head off and wander round and get lost all the time because they were using the underground to get about and of course none of the place names meant anything to either of them, so they'd just ride about on the underground for a bit and come up somewhere random and just take it from there. One time they emerged to see a lot of cars pulling up to some place and wondered what was going on, so they went for a closer look. It was some sort of club that they liked the look of, but they couldn't get in because the doormen thought Dad and George were Ameri-can. They tried to explain that they were English, not American, but they wouldn't have it and didn't let them in. They were devas-tated that they were mistaken for Americans and never found out why Americans wouldn't be allowed into the club.

After a massive amount of work, Pat got the bike ready for prac-tice and Dad went first then came in and handed over to George, who crashed it. In George's defence, Pat did say that he had to use some Araldite to repair the sump and crankcase, which got damaged in the accident at the TT, and some oil must have leaked. Araldite is an epoxy resin that sets rock-hard and certainly in those days was commonly used to repair stuff, but still, it's hard today to think that the bike had been blazing at the bottom of Bray Hill, then mended with Araldite to race at the Suzuka 8 Hours race, but that's how it was then. Honda stepped in again and said to give them the crankcases and that they could seal them, so while the engine was stripped, and the cases went to Honda, Dad and George missed loads of practice.

On race day, there was a typhoon and conditions were atrocious; George reckons he'd never known anything like it in his life. It was so bad that the race got reduced from eight hours to five hours to comply with the world championship status. If it was anywhere else, it would have been called off because the track was basically flooded. Dad started the race because in the small amount of practice they'd had he'd been faster than George, and the fastest one always does the start in endurance racing. Apparently, Dad came in at the end of the first lap and everyone was asking him what was up, and Dad just said he couldn't see a thing. Steve Wynne, who was one of Dad's sponsors, was shouting at George to get on the bike and take over from Dad. So, George did an hour on the bike in the worst conditions ever while Dad had still only done one lap! After about three hours, there were more problems with the bike that took twenty minutes to sort, so they weren't anywhere even near the mid-pack, let alone the leaders. At the end of the race, it was Dad who took the chequered flag and finished the race for the team. George said that he and Dad got a finisher award at the ceremony that night, but to this day he has no idea where they finished. It sounds like the race really shouldn't have been allowed to go ahead, and just finishing the race was a big achievement. I've never seen that award amongst all of Dad's trophies and stuff, and since finding out more about that trip, I wish I knew where it was.

Even though they were uncompetitive, had virtually no practice, conditions were terrible, and Dad really didn't like endurance racing, I love the fact that his skills and status at the time were good enough to take him and his family to the other side of the world. I also love that he was so bloody-minded that even with everything against him he kept going, which ironically is something you absolutely have to do to be any good at endurance racing.

6
World
Champion

think probably the things that Dad is most remembered for are the four world championships he won in the eighties, and his association with Ducati, whose bikes he rode on his way to winning those championships. Both Ducati and the championships that he won looked very different back then compared to how they do now. The F1 and F2 classes that Dad competed in were in their infancy as championships and known as Formula TT. There was also an F3 class, which fell under the same umbrella, and each class catered for different capacity engines. The F1 class was for the largest-capacity bikes with up to 1,000cc four-stroke engines until 1984, when it got reduced to 750cc or 500cc two-stroke bikes. The F2 class was for up to 600cc four-stroke bikes or 350cc two-stroke bikes. The F3 class, which Dad never raced in, was for up to 400cc four-stroke bikes or 250cc two-stroke bikes. The F3 class would eventually be dropped as the number of rounds that made up the championship increased.

The Formula TT championship came about after the Isle of Man TT lost its status as a round of the Grand Prix world championship following a rider boycott of the 1976 TT over concerns about rider safety there. The new F1, F2 and F3 championships were created to keep the TT as part of a world championship series for riders like Dad who did want to race at the Isle of Man and compete for world titles. From 1977 on, the British Grand Prix would no longer be held at the Isle of Man and instead be held on short circuits on the mainland.

Losing its status as a round of the Grand Prix world championship in the 1970s was, without doubt, the TT's biggest threat to its ability to draw the big names and therefore its future, but when Mike Hailwood made his famous comeback to the TT in 1978, after eleven years away, his timing couldn't have been better. I don't remember much about that TT, but I was there with Dad, and I do remember Hailwood's comeback was a massive deal. He was a nine-time Grand Prix world champion and twelve-time TT winner before he retired from bike racing to give car racing a go. By all accounts, he had a very good Formula 1 car racing career with a couple of podiums but no race wins or championships. He also took part in the Le Mans twenty-four-hour car race a few times and got a podium there too. Mike was probably one of the greatest racers of all time and one of those very rare racers who were both quick in a car and on a bike. His comeback to the TT in 1978 was massive news, but you can imagine how incredible it was when he only went and won the F1 race on a Ducati that had been prepared by a bike dealership in Manchester called Sports Motorcycles. Then the F1 world championship was in only its second year, so it was still just a one-round championship – the

63

TT. So, by winning the race, not only was the fairy-tale comeback complete, but he also became world champion and in doing so gave Ducati their first-ever world championship.

By the time Dad won his first F2 world championship in 1981 it had been expanded to two rounds – the TT and the Ulster GP, and by the time he won his fourth F2 world championship in 1984, it was a six-round series, with races at the Isle of Man TT, Assen in the Netherlands, Vila Real in Portugal, the Ulster GP and Zolder in Belgium. The Formula TT format had worked and gained in popularity in a short space of time until the World Superbike Championship was founded in 1988. It took over as the more popular championship for four-stroke bikes, mainly due to using the same circuits as the Grand Prix championship and using production based bikes, but during the eighties the Formula TT format was it, and Dad dominated the F2 class on his Ducati.

When you look at how massive Ducati are these days, it's hard to believe just how small they were in the eighties. Back then they were minnows and Dad was one of the very few people who raced a Ducati at the time – nowadays everyone wants to race one! Dad's first world championship with Ducati was their second ever, and then when he won it again the following year, he was the first to win multiple championships for them and by the time he won his fourth world title, this tiny bike manufacturer had won five world titles in the space of just seven years. They were punching so far above their weight.

Dave Burr sponsored Dad from the end of the 1983 season through to the 1985 season, when Dad's career effectively ended. Dave and Dad eventually became good friends and kept in touch long after Dad retired, and today he's actually my neighbour, so I see him most days! Dave has got some amazing stories about Dad's later years with Ducati, when they used to make trips to the factory in Bologna just before the company was bought by the Castiglioni family, who owned Cagiva. It was that purchase by Cagiva that set Ducati on the path, albeit via a further four owners to become the company that it is today. According to Dave, back then Ducati was only about ten or twelve people in the factory making motorbikes. The site in Bologna was enormous, largely occupied by Ducati Meccanica and Ducati Electrica, producing all sorts, but the motorbikes bit was a tiny spin-off.

In 1981 Ducati produced a twin-cylinder race bike, which was based on one of their production road bikes called the Pantah 500SL. The race bike was known as the TT2, and Ducati came up with it because they wanted to win the domestic F2 championship in Italy. At the time of the TT2's creation, Ducati had no intertest in the world championship, but Dad ended up entering the F2 race at the TT that year on an F2 spec bike that was built by Sports Motorcycles. It was put together by Pat Slinn, who fitted a tuned engine to a Pantah 500SL road bike that had been badly damaged in a crash. Dad won the F2 race at the TT on that bike and in doing so was in prime position to take the world championship at the next round at the Ulster GP. This caught the attention of Ducati, who sent over one of their own TT2s for Dad to use at the Ulster GP, where his second-place finish was enough for him and Ducati to become world champions.

The TT2 was extremely light at just 148 kg all in, and the 600cc engine made about 78bhp, which for the class was good, but its ace card was how the power was spread over a much wider rev range than the two-strokes which Dad had been riding in the British championships and TTs through the 1970s. Everything about the bike was light, small and aerodynamic, and the instant success of the TT2 meant Ducati decided to make some customer versions that private teams could buy, which unsurprisingly included Dad; he, Pat and the TT2 just clicked, and the combination would eventually win five TTs and four world titles in just four and a half seasons.

Dave had an eye on how he could make some money on the back of all the success and push Ducati for a better deal. In many ways he was the dream sponsor in so much as he had a commercial view on the racing and wanted to run a tighter ship for the team but not get directly involved in the racing. I don't think Dad saw it that way; he just wanted the bikes and would do anything to get them, sailing very close to the wind a few times. Dave told me that when he first became a sponsor, there were so many people that Dad owed money to who he had to square up with. Dad operated on a wing and a prayer, packs of lies and bullshit; that approach isn't exclusive to just him – almost everyone in the paddock then and now is the same. He lived in a semi-detached house in Stourbridge with a garage at the side and he had an Iveco van with a caravan, and that was it. He went all over Europe racing with that van without a care in the world.

Despite his love of bikes, Dave had never heard of Tony Rutter before he was introduced to him. They had a mutual friend called Harvey Porter, who raced at the TT with Dad and used to fly model aeroplanes with Dave. Harvey called Dave one day, knowing how much his friend was into his bikes, and said he was going to stop by his office and to meet him downstairs in the car park. Harvey's car had a trailer on the back, and on it was Dad's TT2 Ducati – the bike on which he'd just finished the '83 season and won his third world championship. Harvey explained how he owned half of it, because Dad had bought it but didn't have the money to pay for his half. Dave bought Dad's half of the bike, and Ducati sold it to Dave and Harvey for £5,000.

In 1983 £2,500 was a lot of money, and Harvey said to Dave that he couldn't really afford it and that Dad didn't really know what he was doing the next year. Even so, Harvey bought the bike. Dave asked him if he could afford it, and he said to be honest he'd like to get out of it. When Dave met Dad, he was in all sorts of bother. It turned out that the reason Dad had paid for the bike without knowing what he was doing and without enough money was because of an incident where Ducati had lent him the bike for the Daytona 200 but then he took it to Japan when it was supposed to be in a bonded warehouse after Daytona. He blew up the engine and sent it back to Ducati to be repaired. Naturally, Ducati, knowing that it should have been in a bonded warehouse at the time, started asking uncomfortable questions. Dad never thought past the moment he was in. Dave reckons that someone at Ducati probably realised that the easiest way for them to avoid trouble was to sell the bike to Dad, and I think Dad probably realised he didn't have a choice, so said, 'Yeah, OK.'

Dave and Dad went to Ducati in Bologna to buy some parts for the '84 season and to see if Dave could recover the situation following Dad taking their bike out of a bonded warehouse to enter a race – it was serious. Initially Ducati wasn't too keen on sorting it, no doubt asking themselves, 'Do we need this?' Then Dave pointed out to everyone in the room that they had three world championships and it had cost Ducati nothing – in fact, they had made money by selling the bike to Dad, so I think in the end they just let it go and decided to let Dad have another go at it in 1984.

When Dave and Dad went over to Bologna at the beginning of the '84 season, apparently Dave was really blunt and wanted to get Ducati to stop taking the piss by making Dad pay for his bikes despite winning them three world championships. He just went straight in there and told them straight to their faces that they needed to do better. Dad was wetting himself and couldn't cope with the possibility that Ducati wouldn't budge and he wouldn't be able to buy the bike, so Dave had to tell him to wait outside. Dad was incurable because it was the same story at the end of the '84 season: even though he'd won his fourth world championship for them, Dave still had to remind Ducati of that fact while Dad had to wait outside. By then, Ducati was being taken over by Cagiva, and its owners, the Castiglioni brothers Claudio and Gianfranco, saw the value in what Dad was doing for the brand, plus they had some much-needed money, so for the '85 season they agreed to pay the team £2,500 to go to each meeting. So, with the help of Dave, Dad went from paying Ducati for their bikes and spares to being paid, in the space of one season.

I was really surprised when Dave told me that around the time that Cagiva was looking to buy Ducati, he and Dad had the chance to buy it. They had been talking to them about becoming the UK importer, but then the conversation escalated to them being offered the whole company for £1. The catch was that they had to take on all the debts too, which were substantial. That fact was enough to put them off the idea, but Dave's main contact there, a bloke called Valentini, basically told him off the record not to touch it with a bargepole: as well as all the debt, it was unclear where the racing shop got its money from, which is never a good thing.

That said, the race shop sounds like a really cool place at the time. I think I'd have loved going to the factory with Dad and Dave. The way Dave describes the place makes it sound incredible, and nothing like it is these days. One time, on the hunt for some spares, Dave and Dad were pointed in the direction of the spares department. When they got there, people were flying around all over the place all being typically Italian, and then there was this bloke sitting at a table wearing a suit and smoking a Gauloise cigarette, being really calm. So, Dad and Dave made a beeline for him. The bloke just dismissed everyone around him and said to Dave, 'Can I help you?' to which Dave said, 'Yes, I think you can.' This bloke said in a very polite and formal tone, 'Do you mind if I ask who you are?' so Dave introduced himself as the MD of Tony Rutter Racing, and in turn asked who he was. The bloke stood up and said, 'Please, I'm so sorry. Allow me to introduce myself. I am Giancarlo Dacenta, the Parts Manager. How can I be of assistance?' I love knowing that the parts department at Ducati was pretty much exactly as I imagined it would be back then – chaotic, but at the centre of it a stereotypical Italian bloke, in a suit, smoking a Gauloise cigarette, running the show.

Dave says that the racing shop was an exciting place to visit too: there would be Franco Farni and Fabio Taglioni with another couple of guys working on stuff, and it was just unbelievable. Taglioni was Ducati's chief designer from the fifties through to the late eighties, his most notable design being the desmodromic valve train that uses a cam to open the valves and a cam to close them, instead of a spring. The design is so good that it's still used in all Ducatis made today, including their MotoGP bikes. Farni was a brilliant race engineer and was part of the Hailwood come-back team. As well as being brilliant engineers who were well ahead of their time, Taglioni and Farni knew the importance of racing, so they used to get a company called NCR to help them with a lot of their work on the sly. This arrangement came about because in the early eighties Ducati was a very unstable company and was experiencing a lot of financial difficulties, so the accountant announced that they weren't going to waste any more money on racing and made everyone on the racing side redundant. Three guys who worked in the race department went down the road in Bologna and set up their own company for preparing and tuning race bikes. Their names were Giorgio Nepoti, Rino Caracchi and Rizzi which made the initials 'NCR'.

So, at Ducati you had a handful of guys who were brilliant engineers designing and building race bikes in a bigger version of my shed with the same basic tools due to not having any budget. They had a little test track that went round the factory, and you could hear bikes going past really fast right outside the door – absolutely zero health and safety in those days! The test rider would come in and give Taglioni his feedback, then they would strip the engine, take the cams out and give them to Taglioni, who would be there with a beautiful traditional camel overcoat draped over his shoulders and a cigarette in one of those holders. He would cast his eye over the cams then give instructions to Franco, who would then go off and grind them accordingly, then put them back in the engine to test again. It sounds like it was brilliant, and there in the middle of it all, with these engineers who would go on to be icons, was my dad and Dave – two blokes from the Black Country! When they were happy with the final design, they'd take the engines down to NCR, who would do their bit and then send them back to be put in a frame ready for, amongst others, Dad. He got support from Ducati in '83 with some engines, then in '84 he raced the '83 bike that he and Dave had to buy, but Ducati gave them an engine and another bike to use. Then in '85 they were effectively a fully supported factory team, but as we know a lot happened in 1985, so much so that it gets its own chapter in this book.

Dad did have a go at the F1 world championship too, with the bigger 750cc engine in the same chassis, but he never seemed to click with the bigger bike. Plus, it just wasn't as competitive as the other much more powerful four-cylinder bikes in the class from Honda and Suzuki. That said, he backed up his world championship win in the F2 class in the 1984 season with a third place overall in the F1 championship that same season, behind the factory Hondas of Joey Dunlop and Roger Marshall. Sometimes he would swap the engine from the 600cc F2 spec to the 750cc F1 spec and enter the F1 race, probably because he was there anyway and it was another chance to just race. Along the way he picked up enough points to finish third overall. In 1985, when he got to Montjuic Park, he was leading the F2 world championship, and was second in the F1 championship behind Joey Dunlop by virtue of using a more competitive Suzuki GSX-R750 in the F1 race at the TT to finish second. But for Dad it was always about the F2 championship. If he had any thoughts about winning the F1 title in '85 alongside the F2 title, he would have brought his Suzuki to Montjuic Park, but he didn't. He took the 750cc Ducati engine and swapped it and the 600cc engine between the F2 and F1 race.

Dave and Dad set up Tony Rutter Racing as a business to build road-going replicas of Dad's race bike, but Dave describes Dad as being made of Teflon and having the ability to never get involved with anything. In terms of Dad's overall career, he and Dave weren't together for that long, but they were together for the most successful period of Dad's career ... and his crash at Montjuic Park. Dave had all sorts of plans to make the road-going replicas of the TT2 that Dad had made so famous. He recalls how by his own admission, and even though Dave was (and still is) an active biker, he didn't know much about Dad, so he did some digging and was soon in awe. Dave describes his initial findings of Dad as being a little fella, who went outrageously quick on motorbikes, and didn't crash.

Dave bought Harvey's half of the '83 bike to keep him racing, but for him it was always about the replicas. However, the road-going replica business would prove to be a total waste of time for Dave as he reckons you couldn't find Dad with a radar. He'd disappear, reappear and was so unreliable; he'd just do his own thing regardless of what agreement he'd made with anyone, including Dave. To be fair, it's probably for the best, because while Dad was perfectly competent on the tools he was prone to the odd mishap. One day Dave went to buy one of those kits that you use to rethread damaged threads. The bloke at the shop said to Dave that it was unusual for someone to order the full kit, and when Dave told him that he was involved with a motorcycle race team, the bloke in the shop said, 'It's not Tony Rutter is it?', adding that Dad was one of their better customers because he had a habit of stripping threads. At one stage Dave said to Dad that the painters were coming to the workshop the following week to paint the doors the same colour as the walls so that Dad couldn't find them. Dad didn't understand what Dave was getting at, so Dave had to spell it out to him that he was never at the workshop, and as soon as he turned his back, he'd be gone somewhere else.

I remember calling Dave once when Dad said he was going to do some fibreglassing on the bike's bodywork to repair some damage. I warned Dave that he needed to make Dad stop. When Dave got to the workshop the next day there was fibreglass everywhere – on the door handles, the walls, you name it, it was everywhere. Luckily, it hadn't even set because Dad hadn't mixed the resin properly!

They never actually managed to build even a single replica for the road, which is a real shame. 'We'll get on it straight away, Dave' was always the line, but bear in mind that Dave had come into the racing world from outside, so maybe he didn't really know enough to understand what was involved, meaning that he took Dad at his word when he said, 'Oh, we're flat out and doing this and doing that.' The replicas were how Dave was going to get his money back, but at that stage he wasn't prepared to be firm and say that he wanted a TT2 Replica done by a given date so that he could sell it and start getting some money back into the team. There was lots of interest in the replicas, but Dave never took a deposit; maybe something inside him knew that if he did, he could end up with a lot of angry people wanting bikes that were never going to be built.

The thing is, now that I'm a bit older and running my own team, I see that Dave was in many ways a dream sponsor for Dad. He really wanted to do more than just write cheques out to massage his own ego and bask in the reflected glory of being associated with a world champion. Dave wanted to work with Dad and between the two of them make some money. The problem was that Dad just wanted to race bikes, and in racing there are so many bullshitters that after a while you end up treating people who say they want to sponsor you with so much cynicism that if you're not careful the genuine ones can slip through.

I've lost count of the number of times someone has called me saying he's got £200k to sponsor me or my team, and now I'm a bit older I can hear myself thinking, 'Here we go again.' You want to believe it, but I've had it that many times over the years that when eventually the person won't answer the phone, or they say they'll call me back, I'm not surprised anymore when they don't. I remember a businessman who wanted to sponsor me going to the extremes of doing a really detailed plan for a film on motorbike racing, with famous A-lister actors. The plan even included where I'd sit at the press conference and all sorts, but it came to nothing; they just disappeared. They're absolute nutjobs, and for every Dave Burr (or in my case Bathams Ales), you have to suffer a hundred time-wasters. It's amazing how many people say they've got the money but don't. I think they just enjoy the attention that comes with an enquiry. I mean, what's the point? It's just a waste of everyone's time if they haven't really got the money. But that's how the sport is.

From Dave's point of view, I can see why he wasn't sure if Dad liked him, or if he resented him for the money. It's a strange relationship between racer and sponsor because generally racers have egos, and so do people who are successful in business. I think back to several racers that I know who do resent their sponsors; they hate having to go cap-in-hand to someone whilst thinking they are the world's best motorcyclist. They don't see why they should have to do it, that anyone should be delighted to put their money into them, while of course generally a sponsor will want something in return for their money. But Dad never once saying thank you to Dave is not OK. Having said that, Dad and Dave did become friends after the career-ending accident and remained so until Dad died.

Dad won his fourth F2 world championship in '84 and was leading it in '85 at the time of his accident, so who knows if he'd have won a fifth. Only Carl Fogarty has won as many world championships for Ducati, which is another reason why it's lovely that he wrote the foreword for this book. I'm not sure Dad fully grasped the significance of his world championships; he just wanted to race, and when he got on that TT2 Ducati he was virtually unbeatable for five years. I think that's why it never seemed to register with him. He had a bike that he got on with, and the combination of him and that bike was too much for his rivals, so all he wanted to do was race it and win wherever he could. He would enter rounds of the Battle of the Twins series on his Ducati without any chance of winning the championship due to not doing all the rounds, but he didn't mind. He just wanted to race, and as if to prove the point, when I was clearing out his house years later, I found his four massive original framed FIM World Champion certificates just shoved in the corner of his loft. I couldn't believe it, but it was pretty typical of him. There's no way I was going to just put them in my loft, so today I've got them hung up pride of place in the Bathams Racing workshop, where they belong.

7
1985

In 1985 Dad was forty-four years old and still winning world championship races and TTs. In fact, he was odds-on favourite to win his fifth world title that year until his accident at Montjuic Park put an end to that. When I was forty-four, I had to accept that my days as a superbike rider were over. It had been four years since I'd even got close to a podium in British superbikes, and I was old enough to have fathered some of the riders on the grid! In 1985 being forty-four wasn't such a disadvantage as it is now. Back then, an F1 bike probably made about 120bhp and had skinny tyres, with nothing like the grip of a modern 200bhp superbike.

Nowadays the sheer physical effort that it takes to race a super-bike flat out for half an hour or so is much easier for a younger person than a forty-something. Even so, just look how hard the youngsters all train and how disciplined they are with stuff like their diet just to be able to cope with the physical demands of racing a superbike. Keeping fit enough to do it is a full-time job, and aside from the obvious disadvantage of an older body, it gets harder to motivate myself to watch my diet and do loads of training – not that I've ever taken either seriously anyway!

I was forty-four when I switched to the National Superstock class and set up Bathams Racing. At the end of that season (2016), I won at the last round at Brands Hatch and finish fourth in the championship. I didn't know it at the time, but that was the last time I would win a British championship race. The following season was really my last proper go at a title; I finished third overall behind Danny Buchan and Richard Cooper. Even though I managed three podium finishes that season, I could see the writing was on the wall: my career as a competitive racer was over. Taylor Mackenzie's arrival to the team in 2018 confirmed what I knew deep inside; he joined the team halfway through the season and was on the podium and winning races, while I was on the same bike but struggling to get into the top ten.

In contrast Dad was going all guns blazing into the 1985 season. He'd got himself one of the all-new Suzuki GSX-R750 superbikes to compete in the F1 class at the TT and a factory Ducati for the F2 and F1 world championship, swapping between the 600cc F2 spec and the 750cc F1 spec engines. He effectively used the same bike to race in both championships. He was taking on a brand new bike to stay competitive and entering two world championship classes so, unlike me at the same age, Dad was still at the sharp end.

The first round of the 1985 'Formula TT' world championship was the Isle of Man TT races, and Dad finished the F1 race in second place on the GSX-R behind Joey Dunlop, who was riding a factory Honda. It turns out that by finishing in second place, Dad was the first person ever to get on the TT podium on a Suzuki GSX-R. Since

Fantastic picture of a TT pitstop that shows just how dangerous they can be.

Some pictures of Dads endurance racing. He wasn't that keen on it, but did it anyway

My school playground is the other side of the fence at the end of the garden. Dad kept old tyres in the shed that used to smell.

No idea where this is, but it's a cool picture.

The red and white helmet design got adopted very early in dads career, while he was still wearing "Pudding Bowl" helmets.

Dad was meticulas with his bike preparation, but left the engine tuning to experts.

Dad raced all sorts of bikes over the years.

Getting in the zone.

A well earned drink.

Dads Offenstadt at the
Banthams racing workshop.

The mono-shock rear
suspension was revolutionary
at the time.

This is how British Champions went racing in the 70's.

Dad's van, but with my bikes.

This sums dad up.

Not a care in the world.

Our Iveco van with it's bonnet held in place with a ratchet strap.

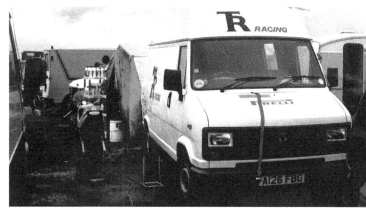

he road to recovery, from broken neck to
eturning to the TT two years later on a
Ionda CBR600.

Dad's left eye never fully straightened, but it did get better than this.

then, the GSX-R has become an icon of road racing and a regular race-winner and podium-finisher at the TT. However, until I sat down to look closer at Dad's racing career, I had no idea he was the first to put the iconic GSX-R on the TT podium.

He also won the F2 race at the TT on the factory Ducati TT2 – which had come directly from the Castiglioni brothers, who owned Ducati at the time – and that would be his last TT win. He left the Isle of Man leading the F2 world championship and was second in the F1 world championship behind the great Joey Dunlop. He skipped the Dutch round and instead went to round three at Vila Real in Portugal, and from there straight to Montjuic Park at Barcelona. He scored enough points in the F1 race at Portugal to stay in third position in that championship and got a second position in the F2 race to comfortably keep his lead in that championship. Then at Montjuic Park the F2 race was first, which Dad finished third in to still be seven points in the lead of that championship. The F1 race was next.

Trevor Nation, whose career overlapped with Dad's for a number of years, was in the F1 race at Montjuic Park with Dad. His Suzuki RG500 had loads of problems at the TT the month before, and Suzuki was looking into them. After a lot of dithering by Suzuki, Trevor decided at the last minute that he'd take his GSX-R750 to Barcelona for the race. However, because it was last-minute, he missed the usual ferry to Spain, so he had to ride the GSX-R all through France, picking up a puncture on the way, which he fixed by putting a screw in the tyre before carrying on. The bike that he rode to Montjuic Park was the same bike that he raced there.

As luck would have it, Trevor was on the right side of fate, and he told me that what possibly saved his own life that day was that his gear lever broke during the race. He was running in fifth

THE LIFE OF A RACER – VOLUME 2

place, so would have been up there with Dad, when the piece of casing that the gear lever hangs on to broke and forced him to retire from the race. He pulled into the pits and half a lap later that was it, there was carnage on the track, and he would almost certainly have been in the middle of it if not for the breakage. Andy McGladdery's bike blew up and dumped a load of oil on the track, and only Joey Dunlop made it through without crashing. Because Trevor wasn't on track when it happened he doesn't know exactly what went off; he had just pulled out of the race, so was probably having a drink of water, or messing about with his bike, but he does say he remembers something going on, that something big had happened. Later on, when it had all been cleaned up, and Dad had been taken to hospital, he reckons no one could find Dad because he was wearing Frank Thomas branded leathers, so when Pat went to find him asking for Tony Rutter, the hospital didn't recognise the name but said they did have someone called Frank Thomas.

Dave Burr was able to tell me more about the lead-up to that season, and the ill-fated road trip which ended at Montjuic Park. Dave explained that the GSX-R came about via a fella called Jeff Turner, who's sadly no longer with us. He owned a bike dealership in Kidderminster called Motorcycle Mart, which years later I would work for before I turned pro. Jeff was a nice guy and unbeknown to Dave he had been talking to Dad and had tentatively agreed that there was a GSX-R coming to him from Suzuki and one of ten engines that had been tuned by Yoshimura in Japan. The Yoshimura engines weren't noted for their reliability as it was a Yoshimura engine which blew up in Andy McGladdery's bike and caused the accident at Montjuic Park – and that was the eighth one to blow up. When you consider that Dad had won a world championship in the previous two seasons on one bike with one engine, and meanwhile there were ten of these special Yoshimura engines of which eight blew up, it's safe to say that they were a bit of a lottery.

All the same, Jeff gave Dad and Dave the bike with a Yoshimura engine, and Dad was free to ride it where and when he wanted to. Dad's F1 spec 750 Ducati (known as the TT1), which he was swapping for the GSX-R, had 105bhp and weighed nothing; according to Dave the whole chassis weighed just 7 kg. It was just three bits of tube, and even now Dave can pick it up and move it – but he can't budge the GSX-R because it's that much heavier. You mustn't underestimate how fast the 750 Ducati TT1 was, but Dad obviously believed the Suzuki was a better bet and that is all that mattered to him, regardless of any agreement he had with Dave or Ducati. I think he also rode the Suzuki because Jeff chucked a few quid at him, not that Dad would have told Dave.

Dave once told me that he didn't think Dad understood how to treat sponsors; he was Tony Rutter and his place was up there, and he had a different set of rules in his mind. I think he just saw the world differently. As Dave pointed out to me, I'm also guilty of having the same characteristics over the years, and in my first book I even admit to being a bastard if I wanted something that I believed would make me faster.

Dad's GSX-R750 never had any reliability issues; he was the lucky one. In fact, a stone went right through the engine via the inlet valve and out the exhaust valve during the F1 race. It did make a mark on the inlet valve, but it made it all the way through the engine and out the other side, which is nothing short of a miracle. Apparently, Dad said he heard it and just thought there was something wrong with the carbs but that it cleared. You know what mechanics are like: as soon as you've finished the race, if you report something odd happening, they'll take the cylinder head off to check things. Dad's mechanic Dennis said he couldn't believe what he saw and showed Dave where it went through, and there it was: a mark on the inlet valve and one on the exhaust valve seat.

Dad was so lucky; the chances of that happening and not seriously damaging the engine are basically zero. He got a second and third at the TT on the GSX-R, one of them with the stone passing through. Even the Italian guys that had been sent over to look after Dad's Ducati had a look at the Suzuki's cylinder head and agreed he was so lucky to finish the race.

The other significant thing about the 1985 season was that at the end of the previous season, Ian Graham – who was the team's other money source alongside Dave – said he didn't want anything more to do with Dad. Dad and Pat were just about to go on the big road trip to Vila Real and Montjuic Park, which obviously costs money, and by then as well as losing Ian's sponsorship money, Dave knew that he wasn't going to be getting any TT2 replicas built by Dad and Pat. The businessman in him realised there was no profit in it, and as much as he had grown to respect what Dad and Pat did with little more than an Iveco Daily van and caravan, Dave also knew it was going nowhere for his business. He went to see the two of them before they set off and told them that he was going to run out of funds by the time they get back from Montjuic Park. He told them that they needed to put their thinking caps on and if there was anything they can do or would like to do that could make the team some money, not to wait until they came home, just to call Dave back in the UK so he could get started on it. The fact was that there was no more money coming in and the team was effectively done, but off they went. The next time Dave heard from them was when Pat called to say Dad was on life support.

In the aftermath of Andy McGladdery's bike blowing up, Joey Dunlop went straight through the pile of bikes and missed them all, then Dad came through on his Ducati and hit them hard, along with about seven others I believe. Dad hit a lamp post so hard that his helmet had split from front to back. He was in a bad way. Pat told Dave that there was nothing he could do apart from deal with the press back in the UK, which he did. Dave also moved me and Mum in with him and his family. I got on really well with his kids Suzy and Scott, and even today feel like part of the family. In later years Dad would just go over to Dave's on his own to spend time there, which makes me think he must have enjoyed being around Dave's family too. Dave had gone from not knowing who Dad was to owning the team, to then becoming a full-factory team, and then to taking us under his wing when Dad was fighting for his life – all in just a few short years.

It's funny – whenever I hear anyone tell the story of Dad's crash in 1985, it makes me think how close to disaster we are when we race. One minute everything is going well, then in the blink of an eye it's all over if you're unlucky, but if you're lucky you just get a big scare. It's even worse when you can see what's going to happen before it does. I was behind Terry Rymer in practice at the North West 200. I thought I'd follow him because he was bloody fast, and he was on the Old Spice Ducati, which was also rapid. We came out of the chicane coming towards Portrush, which is a really fast part of the lap, and we accelerated up through first and second gear. I saw fluid shooting out of both sides of the bike, then I saw the brake lines flapping in the breeze, so he's heading at 180mph towards Metropole Corner, totally oblivious to the fact that he's got no brakes.

He went for the brake, but I knew before he did that nothing was going to happen when he pulled the brake lever. I knew he wasn't going to stop. He was so lucky because he went flying between two people who were turning into the corner and just missed them. For some reason on that day, they didn't put a barrier at the end of the run off, so he sailed through the gap where the barrier was supposed to be and went for ages up the open road before he stopped the bike with just the back brake. I think it was a mechanic just not checking there was enough length on the brake hoses, so when the bike wheelied out of the chicane and the front forks extended fully with the front wheel in the air, the hydraulic brake hoses, which obviously weren't long enough, just got ripped off the brake callipers. Something as simple as that just shows how quickly it can go wrong. Sometimes you're really lucky like Terry Rymer, or sometimes you're really unlucky like Dad was on the 13th of July 1985.

Having moved in with Dave and his family after Dad's accident, I pretty much just carried on with life. Dad not being around wasn't anything new, and while I knew he was in a bad way, I didn't realise just how much was going on behind the scenes, especially the things being done by Dave ...

Dave went to Spain and took Mum. Dad's head was the size of a football; it was unbelievable. He also had broken ribs broken and all sorts of other broken bones – he was a mess. Dave said to Pat to stay there and look after Dad; I think it was about six or eight weeks that Pat was there with him. Then we wanted to bring Dad home, so Dave convinced the Spanish medical people that the English medical people had said that they were happy to bring him home, and the Spanish medics were asking if he was sure, and did he know that Dad had just got pneumonia and was very weak? Somehow, Dave convinced them to bring Dad to the airport so the British officials could take him home.

When they got Dad to the airport, Dave was going in between the two sets of officials and relaying 'messages' while keeping them apart, so they didn't talk directly to each other. The Spanish official was asking Dave if the Brits really did say they were happy for Dad to travel, and the Brits were asking if the Spanish official was happy. Apparently, it went back and forth like that for ages. Dave and Pat even took it upon themselves to wheel Dad in his bed across the tarmac to keep the two sets of officials apart. They got the bed and everything that Dad was connected to onto the plane and secured it in a space that normally held nine seats. Dad was still very sick when this was all going on, but Dave thinks he was aware of what was happening. I asked Dave how the hell he did it, and all he says is he has no idea, and that he was just on a wing and a prayer.

When Dad got home, a brilliant neurosurgeon by the name of Bernard Williams came into the picture. He found out that Dad's C1 and C2 vertebrae were completely shattered. Basically, they are the first two vertebrae at the top of the spine, right at the very base of the skull. Dad had smashed both of them but somehow didn't damage his spinal cord. It's a miracle that Dad wasn't a quadriplegic after that accident; it made no sense. I don't believe in miracles, but along with everyone else who knew the extent of Dad's injuries, I can't explain how he survived and wasn't paralysed. Bernard got Dad straight into theatre and operated on him to put a cage on his head and stabilise his neck – in my first book there's a story about me having to adjust with a spanner at one point. I remember Bernard constantly reminding us that the skull is like an eggshell, which is to say that it can take a lot of force in one direction but not in another, so we were all terrified of the cage.

We all believed Dad's career was over, and even though he came back to racing a couple of years later in 1987, of course the reality is that his competitive career was over. Bernard even wrote a letter to Ducati saying that Dad would never race again as it turned out Ducati had an insurance policy for their riders. Dave got Dad to speak to Ducati and got Bernard to put it in writing so Ducati's insurers would pay out. It was a lot of money, like tens of thousands of pounds, which kept us going for some time. I found a copy of the letter that Bernard wrote to Ducati to support Dad's insurance claim.

From: Midland Centre for Neurosurgery and Neurology

Re: Anthony Rutter (age 44)

26/03/86

This racing motorcyclist fell off his machine at high speed in Spain, on 14/7/85. The accident details were not known to me. He was treated in Spain and then transferred to Sandwell D.G.H., where I came into contact with him and took over several aspects of his management.

He sustained a head injury with a fractured skull, a fracture of the atlas vertebra, a fracture of the right ankle, a fracture of the right femoral head and acetabulum of the hip joint, and there was an old fracture of the left wrist. He was concussed for several days, and his retrograde amnesia was about a week and post-traumatic was over three weeks.

When I first saw him in Sandwell, he had a normal mental state. He had a possible 6th nerve palsy on the right and a certain, quite severe 6th nerve paralysis on the left, which means that he had double vision in most directions of gaze. He had extensor plantar, indicating persisting brain damage. The limbs were normal apart from the fractures. The skull radiograph did not show a fracture basal skull, but this diagnosis is almost certain to count for the 6th nerve palsy. There was forward dislocation of the arch of the atlas on the peg of the odontoid exaggerated in forward flexion. The arch of the atlas had sustained multiple fractures.

I carried out an operation on the neck on 20/9/85 to fuse the atlanto axial facet joints. This was followed by a period in the halo hoop where the head is immobilised.

When I last saw Tony, he was still suffering from the effects of the hip fracture, he still had a severe limp with limitation of hip movement on this account. The left 6th nerve palsy had not recovered, and this means that his double vision is almost certainly to be permanent. His left wrist fracture is still troublesome to him, and adds to all his other difficulties. He has an abdominal hernia on the right side associated with the severe bruising and loss of tissue at the time of the accident. This may also require further surgery in the future.

Tony's injuries may improve in the future, but he would always be substantially impaired in respect of his previous abilities at motorcycle racing. He is absolutely unfit to race at the present, or indeed to drive either a car or a motorcycle or to practise any aspects of his profession. If he has his hip replaced and his double vision problem can be corrected, he might be able to carry out some advisory or other work, but I am still very doubtful about his fitness for racing.

Yours sincerely,
Mr Bernard Williams

One of the conditions was that Dad wasn't supposed to race again, but he did. In fact, Dave was at Mallory Park with me and Dad, and we were watching as Dad came round the hairpin with his head turned to the side. Dave asked me what Dad was doing; he thought it looked like his visor had broken. I told Dave that his left eye won't move, so he has to turn his head to see round some of the corners. Years later, Dave told Bernard about Dad racing again, and that he'd seen it with his own eyes. Bernard was horrified because he said apart from Dad's left eye not working, he couldn't possibly operate a clutch lever, so starting and shifting gears should have been impossible.

It wasn't just Dad whose life had changed because of the accident: Dave's and Pat's did too. Dave had already said to Dad and Pat that in the absence of any road-going F2 replicas the money was running out, so the team was in trouble, and Pat, who had been by Dad's side for so long, suddenly didn't have a rider or team to work for. It was a big adjustment for a lot of people, not just Dad.

Dave still speaks highly of Pat and describes him as one of the most incredible mechanics he ever came across; he was very dedicated to Dad. They really did do their racing on a shoestring, and definitely punched well above their weight; they really were something very special. Apparently, Dave was talking to Barry Simmons, who ran the Honda team back then, and Barry asked Dave how much they spent on racing. Dave told him that he put £80,000 into the team for the whole season. Barry was shocked because compared to Honda, £80,000 was buttons at the time.

Barry did also tell Dave that during that trip, after Dad had raced in Vila Real in Portugal, Barry told him that he didn't know the way to Barcelona, so Dad just said to follow them. So, the Honda racing team, in their massive wagon, followed Dad and Pat in their van and caravan, with Dad giving it the big 'I know the way' routine. Dad took them over the Pyrenees and ended up stuck down a really narrow road at a monastery, with Honda and their 38-tonne truck. They had to back the truck miles back down the road, and it took all day because Dad just left them to it. Barry said he wanted to kill him!

Brian Reid eventually won the 1985 F2 championship by just a few points from Dad, but because Dad had his accident we'll never know if could have got his fifth world title. They were the best of days, and though it all ended abruptly for everyone it must have been really good fun. The 1985 season had some of the best highs for Dad, with his win on the Ducati at the TT and getting the GSX-R its first-ever podium there too, but it also had the lowest low.

The thing is, Dad had his accident when I was a young teenager, so he was physically and mentally a mess for most of my youth. His whole life had changed that year in every possible way. It's inevitable that for my dad, 1985 will always be the year associated with his accident, and I get it, but it's easy to forget just how on-form Dad was in 1985 at the age of forty-four. He started four TT races that June and the three that he finished were all on the podium, with one of them being his seventh TT win. It's funny because he always used to say to me that he won eight TTs and was adamant about it, but typically I never took the time to get him to explain why. The best theory I can come up with today, without him here anymore to ask, is that it might have been the 1976 Production TT that was a ten-lap race with a rider change that Dad and Dave Hughes finished in second place. It was a race that had different classes of bikes within in, and the only thing that I do remember that Dad used to say about his mystery eighth TT win was that there were different classes of bikes in the race, and he finished first in whatever class bike he was riding, but not in the overall result. The problem with that theory is that Bill Simpson and Chas Mortimer, who won the race, were also on a 250cc bike like Dad.

Anyway, the history books will always show that Dad won seven TTs, and that his seventh one was in 1985, but I did decide to have '8-times TT winner' put on his gravestone, so he doesn't come back and haunt me! Some might say that 1985 was also the year of Dad's greatest achievement of them all – he absolutely should have died that year, or at best been put in a wheelchair for the rest of his life. Although he did race again and was able to live a more or less normal life for the next thirty-five years, he was never the same again, so I'm not always sure he saw it the same way.

8
The Pull of the TT

The two years after Dad's accident at Montjuic Park were obviously all about recovering from his physical injuries. His mental state was such that there was never any doubt in his mind that he would race again. As one of his lifelong friends who probably knew Dad better than anyone told me, Dad's mindset was always motorcycle racing, that it was like a corridor with anything coming in from the sides treated as an interference, and I must admit I'm very much the same. For Dad, the massive head injuries and broken neck that he sustained were just interference.

Dad must have had a very high pain threshold because Dave told me that when he was out of danger, in other words when his neck was stable and he could start his rehabilitation, the physiotherapist had him climbing up ladders, doing exercises and all sorts.

The physiotherapist noticed that one of his legs was shorter than the other, which Dad mentioned to his surgeon Bernard Williams at a follow-up appointment, and added that his leg was still a bit sore. Bernard told Dad that if they X-rayed his leg in Spain something would have shown up, but Dad was adamant that it never got X-rayed in Spain. Apparently, Bernard told Dad that he was on life support in Spain and would have had no idea what they did to him, but Dad was certain that his legs hadn't been X-rayed.

Dad got sent off for an X-ray and was told to bring the plates back. When he came back, Dad put the X-rays down on Bernard's desk and started to leave, but Bernard called him back as he was looking at the first one. Dad had split his pelvis vertically and his hip bone had moved 1.5 inches into the pelvis. Bernard told Dave that he must have been in agony, and how he had been doing the physio he had no idea. A surgeon called Nigel Cobb did the operation to fix it; he was the bloke that looked after Barry Sheene, and the operation was successful. He did a hip replacement and nailed his pelvis back together, but that's where I personally think Dad's world started to unravel. After so many operations and surviving so many horrific injuries, his hip still kept popping out, which slowed down his recovery, but once he achieved what he considered to be progress, he started thinking about riding again.

Bernard was a highly respected neurosurgeon who was very highly thought of by his peers, and from what I understand he did a lot of (at that time) cutting-edge neurology research that is still referred to today by people in that field of medicine. Dad was very lucky to have ended up in his care. Dave and Bernard became good friends over the years; I think that was down to the sheer amount of contact they had, especially in the early stages of Bernard taking over Dad's care, plus Bernard was into his bikes too, so there was a common interest. I think also because Dave has lived a much more varied life than Dad did, he had more to talk about and more in common with Bernard than Dad did. Dad's relationship with Bernard was as his patient, and no more.

Sadly, Bernard died in a motorbike accident in 1995 and Dave remembers speaking with him the night before. Bernard told him that he was due to go to the Old Bailey court in London to give expert evidence at somebody's trial and that he was expecting it to be really boring, so he was going to take his bike to make the day more interesting. He had a Honda VFR750, and Dave gave him a hard time for taking a motorbike into Central London on a Friday. The accident occurred in a suburb of Birmingham called Edgbaston during the morning rush hour, when he got hit by a car. Bernard was kept on life support for a while, and Dave used to visit him and talk to him, telling him stories because they thought it would be good, until one time Dave went and Bernard wasn't there; they had to switch off his life support because his organs were failing. He was sixty-four. At the church, Dave couldn't get in because it was rammed full of people whose lives Bernard had saved. It was quite clear that he helped a lot of very unwell people during his time, and his loss was felt by a lot of his patients.

The year after Dad's accident, his Suzuki GSX-R750 ended up in Kevin Schwantz's hands for the Transatlantic races that year. If you're reading this book, Kevin really should not need any introduction, but let's just say he became an absolute icon of motorcycle racing and is still adored by fans all over the world today. It was a race series that essentially pitted a team of riders from America against a team of riders from the UK. There isn't anything like it these days, which is a bit of a shame because it was quite popular and got a lot of interest from the press on both sides of the pond. Schwantz came to England with 'Team

America', which included Fred Merkel, Eddie Lawson, Kenny Roberts and Wayne Rainey. Looking back now, that was some talent, but at the time they were at the beginning of their careers. In particular, Schwantz was unknown outside of America at that time.

For some reason, Kevin didn't have a bike and because he was Suzuki's boy in America, there was a big effort put into finding him a GSX-R750 to use in the races. Eventually Suzuki and/or Kevin ended up at Kidderminster's Motorcycle Mart, who sponsored Dad with the GSX-R that he used in the 1985 TT. The bike was still there, exactly as Dad had raced it, and between Suzuki, Motorcycle Mart and Dad, Kevin used Dad's bike to make his race debut outside of America, and the rest is history. Nobody here had heard of Kevin Schwantz before the 1986 Transatlantic races, but the whole world knew who he was after. He was electric in the races and his unique all-action style was like nothing anyone had seen before as he went on to smoke everyone.

There is quite a bit of urban myth surrounding Kevin's debut in the UK on Dad's bike, so after a bit of backwards and forwards, I managed to interrupt Kevin while he was on holiday to see what he could remember about the bike and his recollection of how it all came about, and this is word-for-word what he said.

> *It's funny – it all came to be when I was at Daytona and Steve McLaughlin came up to me and said, 'Hey do you want to come to England and race in the match races?', and I was like, 'Are you kidding me? Of course I want to go.' So, we asked Yoshi Suzuki if they wanted to do it, and they said no, so McLaughlin said he could find me a Suzuki. So, I said that's perfect. I didn't ask anything about the bike or whose it was or any of that stuff, I was like, 'I don't care, I'm going to England*

to race, and I'll ride whatever was there, as long as it's a Suzuki.'

When I got there, my first memories of the bike were when I walked up to it and McLaughlin said, 'There's your bike', and it wasn't even on a stand, it was leaning against a wall in a building. It had a right-hand gearshift and a load of oil underneath it because it hadn't sealed very well when they converted it from a left-hand shift to a right-hand shift. It also had stock wheels on it, and it basically looked like a standard motorcycle. Needless to say, I was less than impressed – I thought I was going to get a real hot rod or something – but it was as fast as anything on track, and it handled better than anything I'd ever ridden up to that point.

The GSX-R750 came out in 1985 for the rest of the world but we didn't get it in America until 1986, so I'd only had a couple of months on my GSX-R in America before I went to Daytona, and I have to say, I hated my bike – it didn't handle well at all, and I just didn't like the way it felt underneath me compared to the bike that I had raced the year before. But Tony's bike was unbelievable at how nice it was to ride. The conditions we had at Donington that year were snow, sleet, cold and it was raining, but I think we had a couple of dry races.

It was such a well-balanced bike that I remember thinking if I could just take this home, I could do some real damage in the US championship with it. We got it converted back to a left-hand shift and changed the riding position a bit on it for me to be comfortable, and that's all. But wow, it was a real treat to ride, that's for sure, even though I tried to destroy the bike a couple of times! I did drop it at the first turn at Red Gate once, and I tried to kill myself on it going through Starkey's with both feet off the pegs and off the side of the bike being dragged along beside it, then somehow getting back on.

It was that bike and that meeting that got me introduced to Barry Sheene. He was there doing some TV commentating, and he took me under his wing and brought me back in two weeks later, and I tested his 1984 Grand Prix bike at Snetterton and then did the Race of the Year on it and finished second. Then the next thing you know I'm going to Grand Prix at the end of that season, and my career took off. That bike was very, very instrumental in me getting the opportunity that was given to me by Heron Suzuki and Barry.

Back at home, Dad was a nightmare when he was recovering, and Mum wasn't well either, and on top of her mental illness she also used to suffer from vertigo, so it wasn't exactly a laugh a minute. One day when I was at home, Mum fell from the top of the stairs to the bottom with a proper crash; she was in a heap on the floor, half upside down. Dad walked up to her on his crutches and with his cage on his head while I was trying to pick her up, and he just stood there are said, 'Well, Pauline you haven't fallen off a motorbike at 150mph', and that was him. Granted, given his own physical state he couldn't help Mum anyway. Some things he was very caring about, but a lot of the time he was selfish.

He was always short-tempered, even before his accident, and he especially had no patience for people that annoyed him. I remember when we lived at Crestwood Park and a group of people came down the street and started making a load of noise and causing trouble over the road. Dad would be the first one to go out there and tell them to fuck off. Then, the next thing that happened was they came over and there was a fight in the garden. I think Dad must have been a scrapper, because he wasn't afraid of confrontation like that. The next day, he had a crossbow and was saying that he was going to shoot the bastards if they came round again. He was a law unto himself, but then imagine the noise that his race bikes made, the 750cc and 350cc two-stroke engines with race exhausts were really loud when he'd start them up after working on them. Inevitably, the neighbours came round, moaning at him about the noise, and he'd tell me to go and tell them that he'd shove the exhausts down their letter box. So, it was OK for him to make a load of noise, but not others.

I remember having a Scalextric for Christmas once and Dad having a go on it with me for a bit, then leaving me to it. I think that's normal though, and now I'm older I realise that he probably just had other stuff to be getting on with, but at the time I was pissed off with him. He was hardly ever at home, and I've never described our relationship as a 'typical' father-and-son one. If it was to do with racing then it was no problem, which is why I went to as many of his races with him as I did, because he wasn't really that fussed about anything else. Once I fell down and grazed my knee, and Dad just told me to get up, but that was just how it was; it's not a criticism, there's no ill feeling, that was the way of life then, and I think it's as much a generation thing as a racer thing. One person's normal is another person's not normal, and the fact that there wasn't a massive bond between us isn't a big deal; there are millions of others just like that, I imagine.

Having said that, I remember before his accident, when he was well, asking Dad if we could borrow his van to collect some wood for a bonfire that my mates and I were building. We all jumped in the back of his van, like you did in those days, and Dad drove us around looking for wood. We couldn't find any, so he took us to go and rob another bonfire that someone else had built. When we got home, a load of kids came over, saying that it was their bonfire while we were pulling it out the back of the van, but Dad wasn't having any of it. It was his way. It was a shitty thing to do to the other kids, but I saw it as a really nice thing he did for me and my mates. If I were being generous, I'd say that it came from a good place.

It was hard to see him treat people so badly after the crash, especially Mum, but I can sort of understand why he was the way he was. He went into the 1985 season on the crest of a wave, already a four-time world champion and looking like he was on for a fifth title. He had a new Suzuki GSX-R750 to try and be competitive in the F1 class, and a Ducati with full-factory support for the F2 class. He won a TT race and got a couple of podiums at the start of the season too. Dad was in his absolute prime and just getting faster and faster, then in the blink of an eye it was all over through no fault of his own or anyone else's.

He never really cracked the F1 class because he didn't have the right bike. He was against very powerful Honda factory bikes with V4 engines, and his F1 spec Ducati probably only had 100bhp, which wasn't nearly enough power to compete with the Hondas. That's not to say his F1 Ducati wasn't any good – it was a very good bike, the best that Ducati could produce – it's just that the rules in the F1 class didn't really favour the V-twin layout of the Ducati compared to the four-cylinder Hondas. It was the other way round for the F2 class, in which the Ducati was the bike to have, and Dad's was the best Ducati in the class. He raced in both classes mainly because it meant he could do more races. It's not like today, when you race in just one class; Dad wanted to race as much as he could, so often he would swap the engine in the bike between races from the F2 spec to the F1 spec, so it was exactly the same bike, just with a different engine. Nowadays the rules and regulations are always being written to level-up the class, so close racing can happen. Back in 2004 when I had a factory Honda superbike with factory Michelin tyres, the other teams didn't really stand a chance. I had to be really unlucky or really mess it up not to finish at the front, and it was a bit the same in the F1 class back in the eighties. Now it's really competitive because all the bikes are very similar in terms of performance, regardless of the manufacturer. Tyres were just as critical then as they are today, and the big teams like Honda could get the best tyres, but now everyone uses the same control tyre, so once again there's no real advantage. I think at the time Dad was just on the wrong bike in the F1 class, which meant he never had a good go at that championship.

Remembering the times when Dad went out fighting with the noisy people across the street reminded me of when I used to live in Kirby Mallory Village, which is where Mallory Park racetrack is. I seemed to attract the attention of people from the village because I was a racer and the locals all hated me because they've got a problem with noise coming from the racetrack in their village, therefore in their minds I was part of that. One night some kids were outside my house shouting, and I really should have ignored them. Instead, I ran out the door and started chasing them, but they got away, then they came back the next night and did the same, and off I went, chasing them down the street again; I could never catch them. The next time one of them was standing outside my house, shouting that I wasn't as good as Yukio Kagayama, who was also racing in British superbikes at the time and was really popular with fans. I thought to myself that I needed a new tactic, so I stopped chasing them, accepting that I was never going to catch them, and just shouted back to them that they'd got me, that they'd beat me, and fair play to them. They never came back, so I got the last laugh. I don't know why I didn't think of it before because I used to do the same as those kids when I was younger because my mates and I thought it was hilarious to go out of our way to piss off grown-ups and try to get them to chase us.

At the same house, one morning when I woke up, I noticed the garage door was open ajar, then a neighbour came round and said, 'We've caught them.' I asked him what he was on about, and he explained that there were some thieves who'd been into a few garages and stolen some stuff. The policeman who, as luck would have it lived on the same street explained that they'd caught this gang of thieves that were known to them, and they had recovered all the stuff that they'd taken – a few sets of race gloves from my garage but not much else. He also said that they'd left their car round the back of the houses out of sight, so I think this is where I'm probably like Dad: I saw red and just wanted some sort of revenge. I went round there with a load of nails and put them under the car's tyres, thinking that whichever way they drove off they'd get a puncture. When I got back home, I thought that wasn't enough, so I got a hammer from the garage, and for some reason it had my then-girlfriend's name on it – 'Sandrine', in big letters.

I went off with the hammer to smash the car's window. Have you ever tried smashing a car windscreen? It's really hard. I hit the screen with the hammer, and not only did the screen not break, but the hammer bounced back so fast that I hit myself in the face with it. So, I got really mad and went home to get a race glove so I could grip the hammer better and hit it much harder. This time, not only did I smash the screen but because I'd hit it that hard, the hammer slipped out of my hand and landed on the front seat of the car. So now there's a car with a smashed windscreen and a hammer on the seat with 'Sandrine' written on it. I had to break the window even more so I could reach in and get the hammer out – it was a disaster. I went home and did my best to act natural on the way, thinking 'That'll teach them', I was also scared to death that I'd get a knock on the door from the police. After a while, I went back to see what was happening, and the car was gone. I'd never have made a career as a criminal.

Dad used to get the odd visit from his mates after his accident, when he had that massive frame on his head. A lot of the time he was out of it and didn't know if he was coming or going, and sometimes he was normal; he went through hell, but there was never any doubt in his mind that he was going to race again at the TT. It does that to you; racing at the TT is such a unique thing that once you've been bitten by it it's so difficult to leave it alone. The risks are obvious, but that's a big part of the attraction. That said, the Ulster GP was one of the best tracks I ever raced at. It's so frightening because it's so unbelievably fast, and it's a mass start, like at the North West 200, just to really spice things up. Financially the money just wasn't there like the North West 200 and TT, and for me it usually clashed with something, or manufacturers and teams that I was riding for would want me to concentrate on what I was doing for them, so it never really featured that much in my career, but when I did do it, it did scare me. Dad won the Ulster GP five times and used to say it was probably one of the best circuits in the world, even better than the TT because it was fast and flowing, plus the Irish are fantastic and give it a real party atmosphere.

Dad used to say the thing he was the most scared of at the TT was melting tarmac, which he would say was the one thing that you can't prepare for. He said a lot of the surface was really good, but if it was a hot day it would melt, and that scared him and a lot of the riders. It's better now, but it still happens nowadays, albeit very rarely, and if it does, it's usually at Glen Helen – you can see it and it's like oil that comes to the surface. Obviously, there aren't any catseyes on the course, and I'm sure they use better quality tarmac on it than the rest of the roads on the island. After a few days of practice, if there hasn't been any rain, the rubber from the bikes' tyres starts to build up on the tarmac, and the grip levels at the TT become like a racetrack: very high. Even when I first started racing at the TT, the surface would break up, but now it's much better. I reckon if we'd have had the hot weather that we did in 2018 back then, the organisers would probably have had to cancel the race because the tarmac would have fallen apart.

The speeds are so high at the TT that things happen so fast, that they are almost impossible to register. In 2019 the oil sump on the bottom of the engine of James Hillier's Kawasaki got ripped clean off when he hit the big compression at the bottom of Barregarrow. It dropped all its oil just on the exit of the fourth gear corner immediately after the biggest bump on the course. It's a scary part of the track even in perfect conditions, and I was next on the road, oblivious to what was ahead. I hit the bump, then suddenly the bike went sideways, and was on full steering lock, and at the same time I was flicked clean out of the seat. Somehow, more through luck than skill, the bike straightened itself up and just had a massive wobble for the next couple of hundred yards. The wobble was so violent that it ripped the steering damper off the bike's chassis. A steering damper is a hydraulic damper that connects the steering to the chassis to calm down any bumps or weaving that the chassis might pick up. To rip a steering damper clean off its mountings takes a huge amount of force.

It shows how things can change in an instant at the TT due to the sheer speeds involved; it doesn't even have to even be your fault and on that occasion I was a passenger. I do think if I had come off the bike it would have been a big crash, but I think I would have been sent up the road rather than smashing into a wall because I was travelling so fast and pointing down a long stretch of road, but then saying that, the bike could have veered off and I would have been in trouble. My first thought after was 'Oh shit, what about the people behind?', so I put my hand up and started trying to wave to let the marshals know that something serious had happened. Then I thought the bike didn't feel right because it was shaking its handlebars viciously because the steering damper had broken. When I got to the pits I had to retire from the race because the bike was unrideable at race speeds without a steering damper. When you lose control, in that moment you don't really think, you just react, but then in the first moments after the near miss, my first thought was concern for other riders, then I didn't really think about it again. There's no reflection, no what-ifs, no stressing about what could have been. That's how you have to race at the TT.

It's not happened to me yet, but I was really interested to hear Carl Fogarty talk about when he did a parade lap on Steve Hislop's Ducati and how it made him feel differently about the TT. He said the bike was a bit of a handful because the tickover was set really high, so it was running wide through the corners, but it was fast. On the first parade lap, a water pipe split straight away as he was going down Bray Hill, so he had to pull in at Union Mills a mile or two later, and that was it. The next day there was another parade lap, and Carl was due to set off with Agostini, but John McGuinness got the hump and pushed through between the two of them, giving it all 'I'm Mr TT', so the three of them set off and Carl was OK up to Union Mills, where he'd pulled over the last time out. Then suddenly he just didn't know where he was or what he was doing, which is not a good place to be when you're lapping the course, even on a parade lap. By the time he finished the lap his head had gone so much that he was desperate to get off the bike and go straight to the airport. I found it fascinating that someone who had so much success there and was open about how much he loved the place could suddenly and unexpectantly find himself with feelings that are quite the opposite.

I met one of the Isle of Man more famous residents, Norman Wisdom on the boat over to the TT once, and straight away he was so nice. He was telling me that he used to love watching Dad, and he'd go with a pack of sandwiches and sit at the bottom of Bray Hill, and that he could hear Dad's Ducati coming all the way from Signpost Corner, which must be a mile away as the crow flies. He said Dad's was the only bike you could hear from that far away, and the only thing that used to upset him was when people would come and sit next to him and talk to him while he was listening to Dad's bike coming. He said he would try not to sound nasty, but he'd turn to them and say, 'Sorry, Tony Rutter is coming, and I want to hear this.' Then after Dad went past he'd start talking again. He was very knowledgeable and well into his bikes, and it was him who actually came up to me because he knew who I was. I was amazed, but then I suppose I did have my team clothing on. I so wanted a picture with him for my wall, but I didn't want to bother him.

At the time of writing this, I'm starting to get prepared for the 2022 TT. It's been two years since anyone raced there, and even though I'll be fifty years old when the time comes to head down Bray Hill again, the idea of not going back never entered my head. If ever there was a time that I might have considered not racing there again, it would have been during the Covid pandemic. However, I had top sixes in all my races in 2019, so know that I'm that or thereabouts because nobody has been there since. But most of all I still just love racing there. I've really missed it and the build-up to it and getting over there and setting up the truck and garage; it's not just the racing, it's the whole thing. It's crossed my mind every year to not go back, but the answer is always the same, even if the difference is that now there is no pressure on me from my team or sponsors. Now I've got my own team, and also my sponsors are on the same page as me; they know I'm not saying I'm going out there to do this or that. They're fans of the event first and foremost, so just going to race at the TT is enough for all of us. Having said that, I always give myself a goal, and it's got to be a realistic goal. I think for me at this stage the very best would be to get into the top six, that would be like a win, but a top ten is realistically where I might be.

I don't think there will be any advantage for the old boys like me and John McGuinness after the two-year break. Maybe there's a bit of help for us because we've got a bit more knowledge – not just about the track, but the weather and track conditions, plus we've done that many laps – so it might be that we get up to speed a bit quicker. However, the young ones have the benefit of youth, and they adapt fast, so there are pros and cons both ways. Dean Harrison Peter Hickman are fast there, and they've kept racing during the past two years, so they're still going to be the people to beat. However, I remember Dad saying in the film "Suzy and Duke", when he was asked if he could beat Joey Dunlop, he said all he can hope is that he breaks down. The point he was making was that he wasn't going to beat Joey or Honda, but it's 200-odd miles of flat-out racing, and anything can happen. It could be a 10p part, a chain breaks or some wildlife can ruin your race. A lot of the bikes are new since the last TT so are unproven. The Honda is new, the Kawasaki engine has a lot of new parts, and even my BMW is new. None of them has been held flat out at 195mph for three, four or five miles non-stop so there are lots of unknowns, and to win a TT everything must be perfect, even if you're the fastest rider on the best bike and favourite to win.

It is true that I haven't got many more years left, I can't do it forever, but for now I think, as I'm sure Dad did when he was away from the TT recovering from his injuries, 'Why not go and race my bike on the greatest racetrack in the world on a nice sunny day?' I think riding the TT course again gave Dad a lot of motivation to recover from his injuries, because I also know just how strong the pull of the TT is.

9
Paying the Price

My Dad was so stubborn that he very rarely went to the doctor. I think it got to the point in his later years that he had been messed about with so much and been prodded and poked at so many times over the years with all his injuries, that he just lost all motivation to get up and have a normal life. Racing was such a big part of his life, and not being able to do it stopped him from going forward and trying to get better. In his mind he didn't have anything to look forward to, so getting him to go to the doctor when he started struggling to look after himself was difficult. Eventually we found out that he had vascular parkinsonism.

It's a condition that shares a lot of the symptoms of Parkinson's disease, such as a loss of balance, which in turn makes walking difficult, eventually impossible. It's caused by problems with the vessels in the brain that control movement. Often it's a stroke that is the main cause for vascular parkinsonism, but in Dad's case the doctors were certain that it was caused by too many bangs on the head, especially the one he got in the race at Montjuic Park in 1985.

I took him to the doctor a few times to see if there was anything that they could do for it, and they said they could try something but there was a chance that it could make it a lot worse. With all of Dad's injuries and other stuff that wasn't right anyway, they just said it's best to just let him live out his last years. I couldn't believe it; I thought my mum would be the first to go because she was already in the care home, basically just looking at the four walls with not much going on, and I thought my dad would live forever.

Since Mum was already in the care home, Dad was just trundling around the house on his own. After a few months into it, I started saying to him that he really could do with some help around the house, but he wouldn't have it. He was getting worse and worse physically, especially his movement, then eventually it got to the point where I went into the house and it looked like someone had burgled it: the fireplace was ripped off the wall, sort of half on and half off the wall, as if someone had been in and smashed the place up. I looked all over for Dad but couldn't find him, then went to the kitchen and found him. He was stuck behind the door into the kitchen and was just lying there on the floor. He had been there for about a day, I reckon. His balance had become so bad that he would crash into things and fall over, and this time he couldn't get back up. He went to hospital, and they got him fit enough to go back to the house and have a carer to visit him. Then about three or four months later he had to go into a home, which he was really not happy about, but, as I told him, I couldn't look after him and he couldn't look after himself, so it was terrible. On the plus side, it was the same home that Mum was in, so it made visiting them a lot easier for me.

When I went to see him and Mum, it was always difficult. Dad would get very aggressive when I was in there, because he just wanted to leave and go home, which I don't really blame him for. The last time I went in to see him he said, 'Just get me out of this bloody place', and I told him, 'I can't, and anyway, where can we go?' He told me to just get him to the door, so I said to him, 'Where you going to go, then?' All he wanted to do was to get outside and for me to take him home. He really spoke well: his voice was so clear and so easy to understand and it was the best I'd seen him for ages. Generally, by then, his speech wasn't great, and he was finding it more and more difficult to string sentences together and speak clearly, so for him to suddenly be speaking with so much more clarity than he had for a really long time must have meant he was desperate to go home. I can remember too that he was so angry and frustrated with the situation he was in that his fists were clenched. Again, that's not something he had been physically capable of doing for a long time. He was so desperate to get out that, somehow, he managed to muster up some strength from somewhere inside himself to try and get me to take him home. Just for a moment, he seemed well again, he seemed normal. Then he said, 'I'm going to bloody die in here', and two weeks later he was gone.

Unfortunately, I was away testing or something and the nurse called me and said I needed to come in. When I got there, I thought he wasn't too bad and I stayed with him for a while, then left him. The next day the home called again and said I should go in again, so I went in and sat with Dad as he lay on his bed, and the only thing he did was he turned his head and looked at me. It was to be the last eye contact I had with him. I stayed there for two days. During the first night, at about 2 a.m., one of the nurses said I might as well go home for some rest, but I just thought that I couldn't, because I thought I knew what would happen as soon as I walked out the door. However, the nurse convinced me to go home anyway, and promised that they'd call me if anything happened. They were really good in there.

The next day I went back, and his breathing was getting heavier and heavier. He didn't seem in pain, but everything was getting so difficult for him. I think it was just the noise of him shutting down. His breaths were getting shorter and shorter, and he was like that for about a day and half, then he died. I was actually glad for him that his suffering was over. You hear people say things like 'At least they're no longer suffering' when someone dies after being ill for a while, and I really get it now. At the end, each breath was so difficult for him and he was so frustrated to be in the care home and to be so physically restricted; he was suffering mentally and physically, yet he just kept going. His mind was still as strong, stubborn and determined as it ever was, right up to his very last breath.

Dad died on the 24th of March 2020, just as the Covid-19 pandemic was starting to accelerate in the UK, and while Dad technically died on the 24th, it was in the very early hours, some-thing like 1 a.m., so only a few hours after it was announced that the UK was going into its first full lockdown to try and stop the spread of the virus. I missed the announcement because I was at his bedside as it was all unfolding on TV, so it was all very surreal by the time I got home. I had gone into the care home while Dad was still alive, and things were sort of normal in the world, and when I left, he had gone, and the country was in a complete lock-down. Only a day or two later, visitors weren't allowed into care

Dad on his way to giving the Suzuki GSX-R it's first ever podium at the TT in 1985.

Kevin Schwantz on the exact same bike making his race debut outside America in 1986. It was the race that got him spotted by Barry Sheene which led to him riding in Grand Prix.

Dad and Joey in 2000.

Dad and Joey in 1985.

Some pages from dads scrapbook.

Pages from Dad's scrap book.

out it's fairing, you can
ust how compact the
ati was.

Bumps big enough to lift the rear wheel.

Dad's Ducati TT1 at the Bathams racing workshop.

The TT in one picture.

The full factory Ducati Dad got in 1985 just missing a drain cover.

Dad would swap the engine in his Ducati between races so he could race in different classes.

Dad at the Daytona 200.

Dad at the Suzuki 8 hour.

Kenny who sponsored the
trip to Suzuka.

Dad sat in a Tokyo bar
with George Fogarty
who he was team mate
with at Suzuka. Me and
mum went too to make
it a trip of a lifetime.

Dad with his four FIM World Champion certificates.

homes, so I'd just made it really and was lucky to be able to be with him.

Since Mum was in the same place, but a different part, I went up to see her straight after Dad died. She hadn't said many words for the last few months and was also going downhill. I walked up to her room down this dark corridor and when I opened the door she said, 'Is that you, Michael?' I couldn't believe it; it was pitch black, so how could she have possibly known? I sat on the edge of her bed but didn't have the heart to tell her that Dad had died. She was so nice and just like my mum again, so I sat with her and had a conversation with her for about forty minutes, then said, 'Right, I'll see you in a couple of days', not realising that I would-n't be allowed back into the home. At least now I've got a really good memory of her.

But that night it was so strange; it was as though she knew. I went downstairs and told the night porter what had happened and said that it was really weird. He said that they do see some weird things in those places, and I told him that it was like she knew Dad had died. He said that she probably did, and that me coming in to see her at that time of night wasn't normal and might add up in her head. As far as I know, Mum never knew that Dad had died. I would call up to check how Mum was, but I couldn't speak to her because she didn't use phones or anything like that, so I never got to tell her.

Dad's best years were before his crash in 1985, when he was forty-four; it really didn't do him any good. He still came back in 1987 and did bits that he wanted to do but was nowhere near as competitive as he used to be. His eyesight was his biggest problem, and he eventually had to stop racing in 1991, aged fifty, which is what I'll be next time there's a chance for me to race once the Covid pandemic has calmed down. I think if you consider my dad's life and career, he was probably very happy with it all, and I think everybody else would look at it like that too. He was selfish, but he was happy in his head. However, I look at it and think it was quite a lonely way to be at the end, but that's the kind of person he was. He wasn't interested in fanfares or fuss, so it's sort of fitting that his funeral was really low-key due to the Covid restrictions. As the saying goes, each to their own.

The funeral was limited because by then Covid-19 was in full swing, so I was only allowed to invite six people, which was difficult. I'm pretty sure that in normal times quite a lot of people would have shown up for his send-off. I tried to put something together for him as best I could, and I got a few of his mechanics there. Mick Boddice Jnr, who knew my dad well and hung round with him, came along with one or two other people who just showed up and got in, so there were maybe ten in total. We did something different because I know he really wasn't that bothered about stuff like funerals, or how he was going to be buried. He didn't leave any instructions, and we never spoke about it, so all I was sure of was that he wasn't fussed; if he had been, he would have told me. I did the best thing that I thought I could do for him, so he was cremated after we had a short service at the church where his mum and dad are buried.

In 1985 a TV documentary was made about my dad called "*Suzy and the Duke*" and in it there's this bit where they play the sound of his Ducati at full throttle at the Isle of Man TT. We took just that sound of his bike from the film, and played it in the church; it sounded incredible. I was fighting back the tears, which was really hard because I never want to cry in front of anyone, and I nearly did. In one way I actually felt a bit disappointed that I didn't cry, because it would have let out a lot of emotion, but I can't stand people staring at me. It was very moving, and I wish we had recorded it. The funeral director was fantastic; she came to me after and said she'd never seen a funeral like that, with just the sounds of motorbikes. I think Dad would have liked it. We had his coffin in there with his helmet on it, and it was really good.

Obviously, I wanted to bury him and for my daughters Juliette and Cecillia to be there for it, but the headstone took ages because of Covid, and anyway I think there are a lot of people who'd like to pay their respects to him, so at the time of writing this, the plan is to wait until we can have large gatherings again. His ashes were at the crematorium for ages because I couldn't think what to do with them. After a while I thought I can't leave him there any longer, so, along with the rest of the Bathams Racing team, we came up with an idea that we were sure Dad would have liked. On the way to Brands Hatch for the last race of the 2020 season, I picked up his ashes from the crematorium and went straight to the circuit. We kept his ashes in the truck with us all weekend. He used to love Brands Hatch, so we swapped the usual black and gold of my race bike for a replica colour scheme of his red and blue Ducati as a bit of a tribute to him. We also brought his Ducati with us and put his box of ashes in pit lane with his bike and my bike and took some pictures. It looked amazing, and the fans and press really seemed to like what we did. After the race, I brought him home and he slid round in the back of the van for a week or so until eventually I thought he can't just stay in the back of the van, so I brought him into the house and put him in the front room at home until the right time. We got a burial plot for him in Stourbridge, so when everyone's allowed to come, we'll try and do something fitting for him.

The race at Brands Hatch was a massive shock for me. I hadn't

111

raced a bike since the Macau GP at the end of 2019, and Brands Hatch was ten or eleven months later. I knew I'd be slow, so I was happy where I finished because it was better than I thought, but I was so far off the leaders in terms of time. If I was sixteenth and 2 seconds off the leaders that would be one thing, but I was sixteenth and something like 30 seconds off the winner. I was a disgrace! There are loads of genuine, non-bullshit reasons why I was so slow. As well as having not ridden a bike all year, let alone raced one, I didn't have my usual airbag suit, which might sound like a really bad excuse, but bear with me.

I've been lucky to have some amazing kit from Alpinestars over the years, and in 2017 they made me a set of leathers for the Classic TT, when we did a replica of Dad's Ducati. Three years later they were a bit tight, which I'm sure has nothing to do with my lack of fitness; I think they must have shrunk! Anyway, they don't have an airbag, and the thing is, you get used to the feeling of protection the airbag suit provides. If I go out on track and the lights are flashing to indicate that it's not armed, I have to pull in straight away to sort it out. In short, I was worried about crashing without wearing an airbag suit, plus I also didn't want to mess up the replica bodywork, which is probably the first time ever I've thought like that. I've never given a shit about that stuff, but at that race, it was on my mind, and that will slow you down.

It's amazing how your body gets used to racing. At Brands Hatch I basically blacked out on the first day; it really messed up my eyesight for a few laps. I hit the bottom of Paddock Hill, which is a really big compression between the first and second corners, and I remember thinking 'whoah'. Then at the bottom of Druids, where there is another heavy compression, the same thing happened. By the time I got to the straight down towards Hawthorns, I couldn't see anything. It hasn't happened to me for years because normally I'm constantly racing. I was talking to Dan Linfoot, who was riding for us that weekend after he stood in for Richard Cooper, and he said it happens to him too if he hasn't ridden for a long time. That made me feel a bit better and less paranoid about it being my age which was the problem. Once your brain gets used to it, it's OK, but for about three or four laps of the first practice session I felt like shit, like I wanted to puke and faint. Basically, the G-force pushes the blood away from your brain and into your legs, and the only way to get over it is to get used to it, so I just stayed out for the whole session.

It's not just compressions that play tricks with your body; acceleration can be brutal, like coming out the pits at Macau. I think the grip and the heat, and if I'm honest probably the booze from the night before, just sort of makes you not really ready for it, but the first time you give it a big handful it makes you feel a bit sick. Maybe I'm just a massive wimp, but when I was doing track testing for *Performance Bikes* magazine at Mallory Park on road bikes with road tyres, their data logger was recording about 1.2 g of lateral force, which means your liver temporarily weighs about the same as four bags of sugar. Basically, all your organs and fluid are sloshing around inside you when you're pressing on, and that messes with your senses and blood pressure. Years ago, Dunlop got me to do some testing for them, and they made me ride through a skid pan covered in water probably in third or fourth gear flat out with loads of different tyres, over and over again for days. I was going from dry to wet then straight back into dry again, and when I came out of the wet and back onto dry, the tyres just picked up grip instantly, and that would black me out too. After a couple of days of doing that, the body does adapt, but it doesn't get any less frightening when all I could see was a wall of water that I had to ride through at stupid speeds. Still, it paid the bills.

Dad always said he was skint, and certainly when compared to what bike racers have made versus what they've done, he was very skint. However, when I was emptying his loft, there was about £8,000 in rolled-up notes in old race jackets and tins; he just never spent anything, he never went out. I was horrified, because when I was clearing out his house, I must have chucked away three skips of stuff that I didn't check, so God knows how much money I chucked away! I think I found most of it because it was all around the entrance to the loft. There were loads of photos and old editions of Motorcycle News up in the loft; he was something of a hoarder.

I also found his framed world championship certificates in the corner of the loft – one of them was broken – and there were trophies just rammed everywhere. I found some of his old leathers and helmets too, which was really cool. It's quite frighting: that's your life, in the loft, and then it's gone, but I suppose it's a sign of a life well lived. What do you do with it all? I was thinking just how much rubbish I've got of my own, imagining what my kids will have to sort through one day, so I had a massive clean-up too, because I'm also a bit of a hoarder. I chucked out loads of stuff, but still, what will they do with it all? There are bikes, trophies, helmets, leathers, loads of stuff, and loads of it. I must have 200 leather suits maybe. You really do need to make a plan because you don't realise that one day someone else is going to have to decide what to do with it all. I mean, what do I do with Dad's world championship medals, for example? I decided to put his world championship certificates and TT trophies up in the race team workshop, and everyone who visits stops and goes wow!

What's it worth? to some people it's worthless, to others it's really special. I've got some old lap time boards from the TT scoreboard hung up in my kitchen; some of those are original ones from the forties and fifties. The TT scoreboard has just been taken down to be replaced, but for years the way it worked was completely manual and the same way they did it decades ago. Riders' lap times and speeds were painted onto pieces of wood that then got carried by one of dozens of Scouts to the part of the board on which that rider's information was to be displayed, then hung on hooks. It's absolutely brilliant and such a big part of the TT's heritage; I really hope that whatever they replace it with is just as iconic. Ages ago, after one of my races when they were packing everything up, they were just throwing the bits of wood into a skip, so I went over and fished out a few of the ones that were cool. Then I got into the habit after a race of going and looking for ones that are important to me. I've got my first-ever 100mph lap time, there is my electric bike lap record, my personal best 131.7mph and my first lap time from my first 130mph lap – 130.6mph, to be exact; it's cool stuff, or at least I think so.

Dealing with the aftermath of Dad dying has made me realise that I had to write my instructions down and tell my kids what I want, which has changed actually. I don't think I'd like to be cremated. Before, I couldn't be bothered one way or the other – I was a bit like Dad in that respect, you know, just do whatever. Now I think I'd like to be buried in a coffin in the churchyard up the road from where I live, looking over the fields where I walk the dog.

I never really wanted to think about what to do with me when I die, or talk about dying; you try and keep away from that stuff when you're a bike racer. I've seen what the end looks like, and it really is the end, and I really don't want my final years to be like Dad's. I think he was quite lonely in one way. He didn't make much effort with people, and I don't think I'm like that; I like people. I like having people around or going to the pub and talking shit with people, but Dad could easily cope without being around people unless it helped him in some way, which to be fair is probably why he was so good at racing bikes and achieved what he did.

10
Remember to Enjoy Yourself

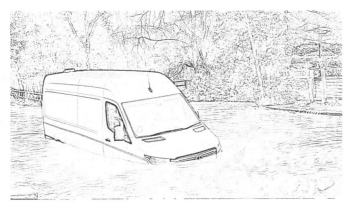

Once Dad got with Bob Priest, he started racing two-strokes and really took to the 350cc engine. Things started happening for him, and virtually straight away he was competitive in the British championship, finishing runner-up at his first two attempts in 1969 and 1970, finally winning his first British championship in 1971, only ten years after he first had a dabble at racing by entering those sprints on his BSA Goldstar for a bit of fun. The following year, in 1972, not only was I born, but Dad got his first podium at the TT, finishing in second place behind the great Giacomo Agostini in the Junior TT. That was the same race he won the following year to record the first of his eight TT victories. He also won the 250cc British championship in 1973, so that period in the early seventies really established Dad as the real deal on the roads and the short circuits.

One person who spent a lot of time with Dad around then was the aforementioned Mick Windsor, a good friend of Dad's and a race mechanic, who also used to tend my grandparents' garden. I know Mick mainly from the TT, but not because he worked on Dad's bikes; Mick used to work on the bikes of Dennis Ireland, a lad from New Zealand, so he was always in the same paddock as Dad.

I remember Dad telling me stories about how people would stop Mick because he looked like Clint Eastwood, which Dad loved because it gave him a chance to wind Mick up. One of the stories was that the real Clint Eastwood was supposed to have been on the Isle of Man for the TT one year, paying a flying visit. So, Dad and Mick were at the Rutland Hotel, which is where Dad always used to base himself for the TT, and one evening one of the girls there was absolutely convinced that Mick was Clint Eastwood. Obviously, Dad encouraged her by confirming that Mick was indeed Clint Eastwood but that he didn't like talking. Convinced, the girl bugged Mick all night, and all the while Mick couldn't speak a word, otherwise his broad Black Country accent would have given the game away. Dad thought it was brilliant. That's how he was – very shy and really didn't like it when the joke was on him but loved it when it was on others.

Mick reckons he found Dad's sense of humour was very difficult to understand and describes him as a complex fella. I think it's a regional thing, and Dad was the master of it. Apparently, my sense of humour is the same as Dad's, as in it's dark and dry and you never know when the punchline is coming. Mick said that Dad had a real knack for timing and at exactly the right time would come out with lines that would knock him over, and when Dad laughed you knew it, because his shoulders would go up and down uncontrollably and his voice was so deep in putting the laugh across it would make everyone laugh to hear his laugh. At the TT once, they went to the Majestic Hotel for a night out drinking and dancing and one of the group fell over on the dance floor and cut his arm. Dad thought it was the funniest thing and just stood laughing. Mick felt sorry for the fella, but because Dad laughed, Mick couldn't help but laugh too, which only made him feel worse.

The grid is a serious place, but Dad was that one bloke who found it funny. Mick told me about one North West 200, where it was pouring with rain so hard that the raindrops were bouncing off the road, then five minutes later the sun would be out, and it would dry up, so they'd all be in their T-shirts. None of them had spare wheels in those days, so to change tyres you had to go to Dunlop and wait your turn for them to do it, all the time crapping yourself because the racing was about to start. They were in the holding area prior to going out on the road and Dad was sitting in there, astride his bike, visor up when Mick ran past him with a wheel to go to Dunlop, way too late to be trying to change tyres. In the middle of all the stress that Mick was going through, Dad shouted at him, 'Fucking hell, Mick, there's smoke coming off the bottom of your shoes. You have no hope of getting there, do you?' As it happened, against his better judgement Mick did make it to Dunlop to get a slick fitted, because it was what his rider wanted.

Then they went out onto the grid to start the race, Dennis having qualified on the front row, and as they lined up it started to rain again, and there was a slick tyre on the back of the bike; totally the wrong tyre. By then, Mick was trying to pretend he wasn't with Dennis because he was so embarrassed and turned around to look like he wasn't part of the second row of the grid – and there was Dad and his mechanic Fred laughing at Mick and taking the piss out of him. He loved that stuff; he enjoyed the daftness of it

119

all. It probably doesn't sound funny to anyone who wasn't there, but when you're there and the rain is pouring down into your boots, and nobody in their right mind would have a slick in for that race, and it's all gone wrong before the race has even started, it takes a certain type of person to be able to cut through all the tension and make it a funny situation. It probably helped that they were from the same area at home and so had a very similar sense of humour.

Dad gave Mick a lift home from the North West 200 that same year, along with Bob Boswell, who was one of Dad's mechanics. His van had a three-seater bench in the front. Bob was driving along the motorway, heading for the ferry early in the morning, and suddenly there was a car heading towards them on their side of the road. Mick reckons he didn't say anything but was sat there getting ready to meet his maker when Dad said to Bob in his dry Black Country accent, 'What do you think he's doing there, Bob?' and they just carried on like everything was normal. Then Dad chipped in with 'Do you think he's lost his way, Bob?' This went on until the car got so close that it suddenly swerved to avoid them. Bob never moved his steering wheel, and the conversation between Bob and Dad for the rest of the drive to the boat was all about the bloke in the car – 'What d'ya reckon he was up to?', 'D'ya think he'd been on the beer?' – while Mick was the only one thinking they could have been killed. Dad didn't bat an eyelid.

Thinking of the North West 200, I believe Dad will mostly be remembered for his Isle of Man and Irish road racing success, certainly more than he will for his British and world championships. In Ireland they worshipped the riders, and they especially worshipped Dad; he was up there with Joey, he had that kind of status. If you were prepared to go over there from England and race on their circuits at the height of the Troubles, they loved you for it. Mick said that they were in a restaurant getting something to eat when word came through that a bomb had been put under one of the seats, and they were told to evacuate. It never went off, but it was part of life then, and like the bloke driving straight at them in the van, it never seemed to faze Dad. Even in my day, when I was racing there early in my career, I would get asked if I was really going to go to Northern Ireland to race, but the people there are so nice, and I never saw or heard of any trouble ever. You could knock on a total stranger's door and ask for help, and they'd give you the shirt off their back.

Mick said that Dad was a man of habit at the North West 200, and on the Friday, which was a non-competitive day, he and his mates always went to the Giant's Causeway and larked about like kids. One year, Fred ended up in the sea after he slipped on a rock, and, true to form, Dad just sat there with his shoulders bouncing up and down laughing at Fred's misfortune; he got a kick out of that. It didn't make him a bad person; he just saw it as being funny. It also made an unpleasant situation more bearable, although he wouldn't let Fred back in the van until he dried out. Fred did get his own back one day though ...

Another tradition of Dad's was on the Friday night after practice at Brands Hatch they used to go to a pub in a nearby village. About eight of them would get in Dad's van, all piled in the back, and go and have a few pints, and on this occasion for some reason Dad had more than his usual couple of pints. They came out of the pub and all piled into the van, with Bob driving once again. Bob decided to take a shortcut back to the circuit via a ford. They had used the route loads of times before, but on this occasion the ford was a lot higher than usual and they only made it halfway across before they found themselves stuck in deep water when the same banter that they had in Ireland starts up.

'What did you do that for, Bob?' Dad asked, while there was literally a river running through the van, with water coming in through one door and out through the other.

'I dunno, Tony.'

'Didn't you see it, Bob?'

'Well, it's not normally there, Tony.'

All the while Mick was sat there thinking how it wasn't really the time for that conversation – but they had it anyway.

Eventually they established that it had been raining heavily and that was why they were stuck. Meanwhile, everything in the back the back of the van was floating, so Fred decided he'd be the hero and opened the back doors and jumped into the water up to his waist. It was probably Dad's tactic all along to avoid having to solve the problem or take responsibility – just talk nonsense until someone else cracks and swings into action. Fred said he'd give everyone a piggyback to the edge, and one by one they all got on his shoulders and Fred waded through the water to dry ground until only Dad was left. Mick told Fred to do everyone a favour and pretend to stumble and drop him in the water, but Fred said he couldn't do that to Dad. Then when he got back to the passenger door, Dad was there laughing at Fred for being wet through again. Fred picked Dad up, and as soon as he got to the deepest bit he dropped him in the water. Dad should have saved the piss-taking until he was on dry land!

Now they had to decide what to do with the van, so Mick flagged down a bloke driving VW Beetle and explained to the driver that they were motorcycle racers racing at Brands Hatch and could he help. The driver had a rope and said he'd pull the van out, so Fred got back into the water to tie the rope to the van and the bloke pulled it out of the river. Then Dad asked the bloke if he could tow them back to the track. There were eight of them in the van, plus the van was being towed by this little VW Beetle, and it was uphill most of the way, so after a bit they could smell the clutch in the Beetle burning, such was the strain being put on it. By the time he got them back to the circuit, the poor bloke had got no clutch left.

Dad wasn't really a drinker, and to be fair I'm the same. I like a couple of pints but not much more, unless there's a reason to let my hair down every now and then, just like Dad. I never really remember Dad being drunk, but Mick does. At one time when Dennis and Dad were both sponsored by a businessman in Dudley, and Dennis lived in a caravan there. One night they decided they were going out for a drink, and Mick was the driver. He had this Ford Granada, and it seems, for some reason, that Dad was on a mission that night and had a good few more pints than his usual. Mick had put a massive sound system in his Granada that blasted out from under the bonnet. He used the car's cassette player to play telephone ringing sounds, as well as a telephone receiver attached to the seatbelt. He would play the sound of a telephone ringing and then would hand the receiver to people at bus stops and say, 'I think it's for you.' Apparently, people would actually take it from him to see who was on the other end. He also had the sound of screeching brakes, which he'd play when he pulled up behind someone at traffic lights.

On that particular night, Dad and Dennis were in the car and Mick was taking them back to Dudley after their big session in the pub. Dad and Dennis had spotted the sound system, so it was game on, and they were spouting all sorts of rubbish through this micro-phone, including a party political broadcast by Dad, which is hilarious to think of because he had no clue about politics. They

123

got to a place called Lye, and at some lights Mick realised he'd made a mistake so reversed back through them, turned left and carried on towards Dudley. By then Dad was doing a race commentary over the sound system when suddenly there were blue lights flashing, and Mick got pulled over by some police. He got out of the car and the policeman was asking what was going on. Mick was doing his best to be all respectful to the policeman and he explained that Dad and Dennis were steaming drunk, and he was just taking them home, and then at that precise moment, the famous saying from Hawaii Five-0 'Book 'em, Danno!' comes out of the speaker at full volume. Mick was just beginning to think he could be in some trouble when a car went past with just one tail light. Being sarcastic, he said to the policeman 'Bloody marvellous! Look at that, one tail light. Why don't you go and get him?' To his surprise, the two policemen turned to each other and said, 'C'mon, let's have him', and left Mick, Dad and Dennis alone.

That era of racing was wonderful, I think, because things were much simpler then, and the racers got up to schoolkid pranks; they really were just big kids and took nothing seriously. It's different now. Everyone was much more together then than they are now. Road racing is still a bit like that, but nothing like how I remember it when I was with Dad. I know that when you're a kid, the sun always shines, doesn't it? But with all the money now involved in the sport and the pressure that it brings to a rider, even at club level, some of the simple pleasures of bike racing get missed, especially in short-circuit racing – that paddock is unrecognisable now compared to Dad's day. Back then they had to find enough money to put some petrol in their race bikes and had no spare wheels or any of the things that every racer will take for granted now. They made their own entertainment and found things funny that perhaps other people wouldn't then or now.

Mick was at my first-ever race at Snetterton, helping Fred, and he recalls how after I'd been out for practice they had a tinker with the bike – not doing much to it, just giving it a clean. Then when it was time for my race, Mick and Fred couldn't find me anywhere because I was off playing with my remote-control cars on the other side of the airfield, having a great time. Mick reckons he came and fetched me, and I spent the whole walk back to the caravan grumbling and moaning which doesn't sound like me at all. When we got there, Mick just said to Fred, 'He's got no hope, that lad. He's more interested in his remote-control cars.' I suppose he was half right.

Mick was about a fair bit in my early days. Dad had retired, and I think my starting up was good for them all as it kept them occupied! I remember racing at Donington Park in the rain – I think I was on Dad's bike – and I won the race by half a lap. Mick was on the start line to collect me after the cool-down lap, so I pulled up in front of him and he took the bike from me. As soon as I lifted my visor, the circuit commentator came over with his microphone and stuck it under my crash helmet, saying, 'Well done, Michael. You did a great job there. Tell the crowd out there how you did it.' All I could say was 'Uuuuhhhhh, I uhhhhhhh, errrrrr, yeah, so ...' I'm sure it was as painful for the commentator as it was for me. When I got back to the paddock, Mick got hold of me and said when that happens again, look at the commentator and say, 'I won by half a lap? Yeah, that's OK. Watch me next time – I'm going to lap the lot of them.' I was horrified; there was no way I could ever bring myself to say anything like that, and I never did, but Mick's logic was that if I did say that, half of the crowd will think I'm a big-headed wanker and want me to fail, while the other half will say what a great bloke I am and watch me try to lap everyone, but they'll ALL be watching me. Keith Huewen and Barry Sheene were masters of bringing attention to themselves. Dad was never comfortable being interviewed or being in front of crowds and used to hide or get someone else to do the interview for him, and while I can't stand being the centre of attention and would rather be anywhere else than talking to a commentator or being interviewed in front of a crowd, I'll do it.

When I was sixteen, me and my mates Alan, Scott and Andrew went to 42nd Street nightclub in Halesowen – I'd never been there before. It was Halloween, and because we got there quite early there was hardly anyone in there, just around fifty people. Then someone said we should have a dance, and I am just not one for dancing as I can't bear the thought of being the centre of attention. My friends all started to dance, and I was the only one not dancing, so after a while I thought I'd be better off joining in to blend in because I'd become the odd one out. So, I started dancing and said to one of my mates, 'Look at them girls laughing. I wonder what they're laughing at', and he said, 'They're laughing at you!' So that was it for me; it was the first and last time I've ever danced. I'm still mentally scarred from that experience.

It's strange that I can worry so much about people looking at me on the dance floor and about what they think about me but not give a stuff about riding a motorbike in front of tens of thousands of people all looking at me. Having said that, I remember when British Superbikes changed the qualifying format to 'Superpole', which was basically when you went out on your own and had the track to yourself, so there was no possibility of getting held up or in someone's way. It really spooked me at Donington Park for the first 'Superpole' in 2001; as I went over the start/finish line to start my lap I realised everyone was watching me, on the basis that I was out there on my own. Suddenly I started thinking differently and worrying about making a mistake. I remember getting good drive out of Goddards, which is the corner that leads onto the start/finish straight to start the lap, and all I could think of was how embarrassing it would be if it went wrong. I went into the first corner – Redgate – and gave it a massive handful of throttle on the Kawasaki that I was riding and got a big slide, which pitched me out of the seat. I landed back on it, somehow going in the right direction, and I remember thinking that I'd blown it. That happened just because I was worrying more about people watching me than the task at hand. As it happens, I qualified in second and just missed out on pole position. When there are loads of us out there at the same time racing, I just assume no one is looking at me or interested in looking at me. Admittedly, at the TT you're on your own out there, but I'm just too scared there to think about anything like that.

The thing about remembering to enjoy yourself isn't just to say treat it all as a laugh and don't take any of it seriously. I learned from Roger Marshall early on that enjoying it also makes you faster; in fact, it was in my first season as a pro when I raced a Kawasaki for the Medd team in 1993 that I learned that lesson. There were quite a few problems with the team, which, looking back now, were probably due to everyone being very inexperienced at the time, hence why Roger was brought in as team coordinator. Working for Stuart Medd wasn't easy at the time; he'd never raced himself and he was very opinionated. I remember when I went to my first TT in 1994 on the Medd Honda RC45, and during my first-ever lap of the course my brake lever fell off, so it had taken half an hour or something to get back to the pits, because I had no brakes. I'd just about survived and cheated death on my first-ever lap of the most dangerous racetrack in the world, and all I got was a bollocking! Then in the race my rear wheel cracked, and I was lucky it didn't fall apart, unlike my teammate Robert Dunlop, who suffered a really bad accident when his rear wheel broke apart in the race.

At Cadwell Park I was watching a practice session, and Roger pulled me to one side and asked me if I really wanted to do this, and if I was really motivated. He had a proper good chat with me and pushed me hard on what it was I was doing. Then we went to Mallory Park, and massive things changed. The biggest change was Roger taking me and my teammate Ray Stringer out for a few pints in Mallory Village to let our hair down, and we both went 0.5 seconds quicker the next day. The lesson was to enjoy racing. As Roger said, you've got to enjoy it. People like Dani Pedrosa are so serious, and they're never going to be world champion because there's no relief valve. Look at the likes of Rossi, Marquez, Quartararo; they've all got smiles on their faces all of the time, just loving their racing.

Roger said that it took Wayne Gardner three years to take the British title off him, on his way to having an amazing career and becoming 500cc world champion. Wayne had tried a sports psychologist and all that stuff, but after two years of struggling he called Roger and asked if he would go to the Dutch GP with him because he had completely lost his way. Basically, Roger went there and took Wayne into Assen on a massive piss-up that ended up with them putting a hire car into a dyke on the way home. Wayne's wife Donna was waiting with the rolling pin when he got back to the motorhome, and of course Erv Kanemoto, who was Wayne's crew chief, was also waiting for him, very upset at what had taken place. Wayne woke up the next morning with a hangover, so he got some pills into him, and Roger told him he had to start enjoying himself again, like they used to when they were teammates in Britain. Wayne qualified on pole, won the race, and started messing about and wheelying scooters around the paddock, having a beer again, and the following year he won the world title. Roger didn't have to be a sports psychologist to know what made Wayne tick; having a laugh and a beer isn't for everybody, but the point is there has the be a relief to the pressure.

Roger did make me laugh when he said that he had taken me and Ray to Cleethorpes Beach and got us running and doing sit-ups and all sorts. He was shocked at how unfit we were. I think I've blocked that out, as I do with any form of exercise that I'm made to do; I can't remember any of that on the beach, but it must have been depressing for Roger, who by then had been retired a couple of years and was still fitter than me and Ray, who were in our twenties. He must have been thinking, 'What am I going to do with these guys?' I've got a lot of time for Roger; he had a really positive impact on my career at a time when I needed it. Plus, he's still in the paddock working with riders young and old, and at the time of writing he's working for the McAMS Yamaha team with their riders too, and I'm willing to bet I know what his fundamental message is to them still – remember to enjoy yourself.

11
Respect

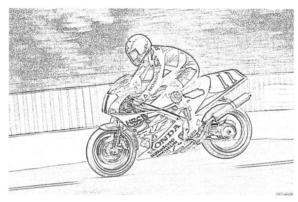

When I visited Carl and George Fogarty to see what they remembered about Dad, it was great to hear George especially recall some of his memories of his time spent racing against Dad. It was also a real treat to watch and listen in to George and Carl reminiscing about their days together when Carl used to go along to watch his dad race, and then later when George supported Carl as he started out racing. Both of them had some stories about Dad, but it was also their conversation about their memories of each other that I found just as fascinating. It reminded me that Dad and I never really spent any time sharing our memories of each other. To be honest, we didn't do much together, or have that much interest in each other's lives, which I regret today. George and Carl were great, and both of them are seriously knowledgeable and have amazing abilities to recall events that took place decades ago. I can barely remember what I did last week.

Even though George is as sharp as a pin and very able to recall things, he claims that his memory isn't great because he was knocked out twice in his career. On one occasion, in 1977, he fractured his skull and was unconscious for two weeks. The accident was at Croft in a British championship race, when he was dicing for the race win with Roger Marshall. He got taken to Bridlington Hospital, and then to Hull Hospital, where he came to two weeks later just as his brothers arrived from Blackburn to visit him. Apparently, George saw an opportunity for a lift home and said he'd go home with them. The doctor said he couldn't go unless he discharged himself, so he filled in the forms and went home!

A year later George went testing with Mike Hailwood, and it was the first time he'd been on a bike since the accident. Mike fell off the Ducati at some point and injured himself, so George had to do the bulk of the testing for him. Turns out that they were trying different bikes, and one had the gearshift set in the race pattern, when you push it down to change up and pull it up to change down, and the other had it in the road pattern, which is the opposite. Mike lost track of which bike he was on, and when he went for a higher gear on it he actually got a lower one, so it locked up and flicked him off. It's an easy mistake to make when you're constantly swapping between bikes with different shift patterns, and it proves that Mike was human after all!

George came to know Dad in the early sixties, and he thinks they first met at Oulton Park. George started racing in 1959, a couple of years before Dad did, and he did his first TT in 1966, which was Dad's second TT. George finished twelfth in the Junior race and thirteenth in the Senior race, so he scored world championship points on his debut. Dad was in the same races as George but finished twenty-sixth in the Junior and retired from the Senior. Thinking about it, finishing and scoring championship points on your TT debut in both races is really special, so big respect to George.

Knowing how good a rider George was in his day made it even nicer when he went on to admit that until he read some articles about Dad some years later he didn't realise how good Dad was. He reckons Dad was the only rider in fifty years who won the 250cc race, the 350cc race, the 500cc race and the 1,000cc race at North West 200 and held the lap record in each class at one time or another. He was adamant that Dad also held the lap record at every track on the British Isles at one time or another during his career, and reckons that Dad was unbeatable on the roads because of the sheer number of places that he won and the classes he won in. Apparently, when George was told that Dad was going to be his teammate for the Suzuka 8 Hours race in 1982, he was over the moon and told the team If he could have picked his own team-mate out of anyone, it would have been Dad.

The more I heard George talk about Dad, the more I started to realise that they got on really well and were good mates. George would talk to other riders like Roger Marshall and Steve Parrish, but Dad was the only one George really socialised with for a while – despite him being a character off the track and a tough guy on it. Turns out they also did some business over the years, with Dad selling George some of the bikes that he'd finished with, and Carl thinks Dad might have been the one who sold him his first race bike.

George and Carl both said that they always tried to buy Dad's bikes because he was good at setting up his two-stroke engines. Apparently, Dad's TZs were so well prepared and tuned that he was the man to go to if you wanted to buy a quick, reliable race bike. This went on for a few seasons until 1976, when George used an ex-Alex George race bike for his '77 season. He was surprised to learn that Dad didn't actually do any of the tuning work on his engines and really just worked on the chassis and maintenance. As I said earlier, Dad was lucky to cross paths with Fred Hagley from Omega Pistons early in his career, because not only did Fred live nearby but he was one of the very best in the business when it came to setting up and tuning engines; it's why Dad got him involved. Just like every racer that there ever was, Dad used to spend every single penny he had on bikes, and everything he bought for the bike was always brand new, which George agrees is the best way to be sure. George used to buy used parts and admits you really don't know what you're getting.

Dad always seemed to have very reliable bikes, and as Carl said, back then a lot of the circuits had really long straights, so if you had a good engine, especially the two-strokes, it could make it a lot easier. If its carburation set-up is too rich then it won't go fast enough, and if it's too lean then it seizes. I think Dad knew that too.

George also bought Barry Sheene's Suzuki 750cc triple, which as you can imagine he really wishes he still had today. Apparently, it had *Barry's Flyer* engraved on the engine's barrels, and Carl was quick to remind his dad that he finished second behind Joey Dunlop on that bike when Joey scored his first TT win in the 1977 Jubilee TT. That was George's one and only TT podium. In contrast, the 1977 TT was a shocker for Dad; he retired from all four races that he entered.

Carl said he doesn't really remember much about Dad, only that George used to buy his bikes from him, and how as a kid seeing Dad's bikes was really exciting. He really liked Dad's colours and thought they were cool, so much so that whenever one of Dad's bikes would come to them, George would just leave it in Dad's colours. Carl's first bike came through Dad: though it wasn't one of Dad's it was sourced by him so that George could give it to

Carl for him to start racing in 1984. I remember being at Oulton Park with Dad that year, and it was a big thing that George Fogarty's son had started racing. Carl is a few years older than me, so we never really raced against each other that much. By the time I started, he'd already got five seasons under his belt and had moved on.

George stopped racing in 1983 so he could help the then eighteen-year-old Carl. Carl remembered racing one of his dad's bikes, which used to be one of my dad's F2 Ducatis, in his first-ever race, oblivious that he was basically cheating because George had entered Carl into the 500cc class on a 600cc bike! George's logic was that the only other class he could enter Carl into was the 1,200cc class, which he stood no chance in on the 600cc Ducati. The Ducati had an electric start so only needed the push of a button to fire up the engine, but George told Carl he couldn't use the electric start, because the races were started with bump-starts back then. However, no matter how hard he tried, Carl just couldn't bump-start that bike, and because it was Carl's first-ever race he was really nervous, plus he had drawn grid slot 36 out of a hat so was right at the back of the starting grid. The whole family had turned out to watch Carl's first race, so to avoid the embarrassment of not being able to bump-start the Ducati, Carl just pressed the starter button and got going. The problem was that he did it so early that he was in the lead before the starter had dropped the flag. Carl finished second but inevitably got disqualified, despite George claiming the electric start didn't work on the bike, so for the next race the organisers sent someone to watch Carl at the start.

Carl started the next race on the second row, and this time when the starter's flag dropped Carl started pushing like mad and pretended to bump-start the bike, but he just pushed the starter button as soon as he jumped on to make it look like a successful bump-start. He got away fourth and by his own admission was riding wild, on the grass, all over the place, and not using any 'normal' lines. He won the race and was understandably thrilled to bits, but then the bike got protested for having too big an engine, so Carl got disqualified twice at his first race meeting because of one of Dad's ex-race bikes.

It was strange to hear Carl and George reminisce about a trip they made to Montjuic Park in Spain for the 1976 Spanish Grand Prix, when Carl was twelve years old. Montjuic Park is a place that is, for all the wrong reasons, associated with Dad because he nearly lost his life there, so it was a surprise for me to hear Carl and George talk about how Carl nearly died there too. It was the only Grand Prix that George did outside of the UK, and he eventually finished twelfth. However, it was also Carl's first-ever trip abroad for a holiday, and he nearly drowned. George and his mechanic were at the circuit and Carl was at the beach with his mum and sister. Unbeknown to his mum, Carl was in the sea and got flattened by a big wave then found himself being taken out to sea. When he described what happened it made my blood run cold; he was in real trouble, up and down, trying to grab some air, then back under the water, struggling to get back up for more air. He says he remembers thinking, 'Is this it?', but luckily a stranger spotted what was going on and went out to rescue him. When they got back to the beach, Carl was semi-conscious and coughing up loads of water. They didn't need to resuscitate him, but he had to go to hospital to get checked over. George only found out what had happened when he got back from practice at the circuit.

Carl was obviously one of his dad's biggest fans when George was racing. One of the international race meetings at Scarborough stands out for Carl as a lot more traumatic for him than it was for

135

his dad. George was racing a Ducati and described it as the best Ducati he ever rode, saying it did everything he wanted it to do. He was leading Steve Tonkin and Phil Read until the last corner of the last lap when he dropped it, believing that Steve Tonkin was making a last-corner lunge on him. His instinct was to stay out wide, off the racing line, expecting Steve to come sailing through and miss the corner, only to drop it himself. George was able to pick it up and still finish in third place and to this day he remains philosophical about it and prefers to remember how nice the bike was to ride and how he really enjoyed the racing. In contrast, Carl was gutted about his dad not winning the race and says there was a spectator next to him taking the piss out of George. Carl was witness to the comments this bloke was making about his dad and was devastated at what had just happened and what he was also hearing, so he just started crying his eyes out, while really wanting to punch the bloke's lights out.

Apart from his podium in 1977 George didn't have much luck at the TT, retiring from twenty-seven of the forty-two races that he started there, which really is unlucky. Then again it could be said that George was very lucky, given that a lot of his retirements were crashes, which at the TT are a roll of the dice when it comes to whether you survive or not. George's bad luck and crash record at the TT seems to have become a bit of a family joke, and there's banter between Carl and George about it, with Carl saying that if you go round the circuit with his dad all you'll hear is 'I crashed there, and I crashed there, and there, and there and there.' George can laugh about it now and recalls another time when he crashed his Yamaha TZ350 at Glen Helen after it seized. The helicopter came for him again and when George was put in it the pilot turned and said, 'Hello George, here again!' He was on first-name terms with the pilot!

On another occasion he was lying in second place behind Phil Read at the end of the second lap but got a hole in his radiator and had to retire. In 1978 George's Moto Guzzi just stopped straight away with a flat battery on Bray Hill at the start of the race. The year after his podium finish George got to start at number one – it's a big deal to be first on the road, and Carl told me that he was dead proud seeing his dad set off first. However, it didn't last long: his chain came off at Quarter Bridge, which is about a mile into the race. A mechanic hadn't tightened the back wheel up and even though Carl was a kid, he remembers being so angry. Then in 1980 or 1981 George was running in second place behind Mick Grant, and Carl found a piece of slate and wrote 'P2' on it to show George at Signpost Corner, near the end of the lap, only to hear 'George Fogarty has crashed'; Carl was distraught. There had been a rain shower at Bradden Bridge that caught George out, but, as George says today, he crashed and survived while another lad from Australia lost his life in the same rain shower. Luck takes on different forms.

For the 1979 TT, Mike Hailwood got to choose between the Sports Motorcycles factory Ducati that he'd finished fifth with in the F1 race, or the new Suzuki RG500 for the Senior race. He chose the Suzuki, which Dad also used in that race to finish second to Mike. That meant the Ducati that Mike didn't choose for the Senior went to George, who then promptly smashed it to pieces at Signpost Corner. He went straight into the banking and there were bits of bike everywhere!

Another lucky escape for George was when he set off with Mike Hailwood in his comeback year; he was number 11 and Hailwood was 12. George reckons his bike was faster than Mike's and that his brakes felt strange but was able to make up lots of time on Mike while braking. They were together on the road until

George's bike seized at Ballacraine. When George parked up, a marshal said there was something wrong with his front wheel, and when George investigated he found that his brake pads had been fitted the wrong way round, so he pretty much had no brakes. Carl reckons that's why his dad was going well!

I remember being out the back of the pits at the TT in '82 and seeing smoke from a fire somewhere on Bray Hill, and it was George. He went missing and no one could find him because there was so much smoke, fire, carnage and people panicking about where he was. My dad told me they found George in a pub, but George set the record straight, telling me how he remembers sliding down the middle of the road and there being loads of smoke. When he came to a stop, someone pulled him onto their driveway, and he just stayed there for a while. The bike was burnt out after the crash, and George had to miss the Senior race on the Monday because his hands were damaged from trying to stop himself while he was sliding down the road. The nurse at the hospital was a bike-racing fan and treated his hands every day, so he got passed as fit to ride in the F2 race; he finished 5th and Dad won.

It was that bike that Dad and George shared when they raced at the Suzuka 8 Hours endurance race next. It needed loads of work doing to it but there was no time, so it got shipped to Tokyo and fixed up there. The Suzuka trip was towards the end of George's career and was funded by some guy called Kenny. George remembers meeting him, but like Carl, and everyone else it seems, he has no idea what he did or where his money came from, only that he had plenty of it and paid for everything at that Suzuka race. The bike just had 'Kenny's' on the side, which didn't help anyone know what he did. George's hands were still not right after his Bray Hill crash, but another crash in practice at Suzuka broke his scaphoid and he needed a bone graft when he got home.

I was able to go on that trip to Japan with Mum and Dad; Carl reckons he probably had to stay home because he was doing his exams or something. The plane stopped somewhere in Alaska to refuel and somehow George's leathers went missing, which became a bit of a joke, with everyone saying that because one of the engines broke down, they had to use George's leathers to wedge into the engine to stop an oil leak so we could make it to Japan. He got himself a new set when he got there.

Dad and George used to travel together a lot more than I really appreciated at the time. They travelled to Vila Real in Portugal once, which is a road circuit through towns, across railway lines and all sorts. The first time George and Dad went there they had a drive round in a car to learn the track together, and when the race came Dad won it and George had to retire from it with an oil leak. However, George's lasting memory of that race was how hot it was: apparently it was so hot that even Dad, who never complained about anything like that, said after the race, 'Eeee, that was hard work.' The heat was getting too much for George and he was struggling a lot with it, but all Dad would say is that it was getting on top of him a bit. He never liked to let on if he was suffering or in pain.

George remembers Ducati sending a pair of their 600cc TT2 F2 bikes for him and Dad to use at the Ulster GP in 1981. At the same time, another van came with a pair of 750cc TT1 F1 Ducatis for some Italian riders to race. Dad did two laps, taking them round the circuit in their car, showing them which way it went, then left them to carry on learning the circuit. After the first practice session the next day, the Italians did two laps each, came in and said, 'Forget it, we're going home.'

Listening to George talking about the times he shared a track with Dad got me and Carl remembering the time we raced each other.

We didn't race each other many times in our careers, but there was the 1997 round of the World Superbike Championship, when I got a wild card entry and Carl was at the peak of his World Superbike career, pulling in over 100,000 people to Brands Hatch that year. I've got my memories of that day and have never spoken about it with Carl, so it was good to hear how he remembers it.

He recalls that I had been there a few weeks before with the British championship and raced in the wet, and the race that day was also wet. He had thrown away the first race which he should have won due to being impatient to get past Neil Hodgson and John Kocinski. He highsided at turn 2 and took Simon Crafar and Pierfrancesco Chili with him.

The second race started dry but got stopped due to rain and Carl had about a four-second gap to Kocinski, which was all that mattered to him. He remembers getting away first in the restart, and being a bit nervous because he didn't believe he was that good in the wet. He said that I came past, and he thought, 'No problem, let him go, I've no interest in him.' Then Kocinski came past him and he was quick in the wet, so he thought, 'You know what? Fuck this, I'm just gonna go for it.' So he just let go of all the worry and followed Kocinski, and it was probably the best he ever rode in the wet. He was third on track, Kocinski hadn't beaten Carl on track by enough to overturn the four-second gap from the dry part of the race, and I was first on track, third on aggregate.

It was Carl's first year back at Ducati, and they had gone to using a single fuel injector, which made it a difficult bike to ride, but he was getting away with it that season. Kocinski was getting stronger through the season because was so good in the wet, and for some reason there were a lot of wet races that year, which kept him in it. Kocinski won the title by twenty points, so Carl points to that race 1 crash at Brands Hatch as the thing that hurt him the most for the title. It was the last time he won at Brands Hatch, and he told me that he'd rather have crashed out of that wet race than get beaten by Kocinski.

I remember being at the TT in 1991 with Dad; it was his last one, and he was using the little Suzuki RGV250 that I was racing at the time. It was also the year that Honda went to the TT with a pair of really trick full-factory RVF750s to spoil some sort of Yamaha anniversary. They also got the best two TT riders at the time to ride them, just to make sure: Carl, and Steve Hislop. I remember standing next to the RVFs in the warm-up area; they were amazing, and I wondered what they must have been like to ride, so I took the opportunity to ask Carl while I had the chance.

Carl did one race on that bike and had to share it in practice with Joey because he had to fly off and race in the American round of World Superbikes on an RC30, which was sort of the poor relation to the RVF. In the end he didn't get enough time on it in practice due to sharing it and there being a few wet sessions, which meant he never really got to grips with it. On the first lap of the race the RVF cut out early on, so by the time he got to Ballacraine he was already 5 seconds down on Steve. The bike behaved itself to Ramsey, so he was still 5 seconds down on Steve at that point, then it cut out again for a few seconds on the approach to Brandish, which is a really fast section on the way down the last bit of the mountain section. On the second lap it cut out completely on the run down to Ballaugh Bridge and he was pulling in to retire from the race when it fired back up just as Steve passed him.

Steve had started 30 seconds behind Carl on the road, so by

making that up and passing Carl Steve obviously has got the race in the bag. However, Carl caught him up and passed him on the mountain to lead on the road, albeit with Steve leading Carl by 30 seconds on corrected time. The pictures of the two of them on the road together were a dream for the Honda marketing department. Then Carl's bike cut out again, this time coming out of the super-fast Brandish, and Steve just missed him. During the pitstop Steve was shouting at his crew, 'He's tried to knock me off', and Carl was trying to tell Steve that his bike was cutting out. Pitstops at the TT are stressful enough without riders arguing with each other, so I can only imagine what that would have been like for the pit crew. Then the bike wouldn't start after the pit stop, so he lost more time to Steve, but on the fifth lap it didn't cut out once and he says it was the first time he felt like he was at one with the bike and started to catch Steve again.

He could see Steve in the distance, and thought to himself, 'Right, fuck it. I'm gonna smash the lap record to pieces here on the last lap', and off he went on a mission. One of his mates was watching on Bray Hill and said that Carl didn't shut the throttle from the top to the bottom; he was flying on the thing, going faster than he'd ever gone, then on the run down to Ballacraine it cut out for long enough for Carl to be all the way back to first gear in a place you're usually in sixth gear. Then, you guessed it, it fired up again and he finished the lap and finished second. Carl is adamant that the lap would have easily been an average of 125mph because he did a 123mph lap the year after, and he is certain that the lap in '91 on the RVF was miles faster. I know what he means; you just know when you're on a good lap. My personal best lap at the TT is 131.7mph, which I did in 2017, but there's no doubt in my mind that I've done faster laps that I've been held up on at the end or something like that, which just takes it away from you.

They found that a loose wire on the kill switch was causing it to cut out, but Carl got to ride the same bike later that year at the Suzuka 8 Hours race and finished third. He said it was a beautiful bike to ride, and because it was a prototype it just dripped in exotic materials, and details and that given the chance he'd love to own it, which was interesting to hear. There are one or two bikes that I've raced over the years that I'd love to own, but I'm also keen to try and buy some of Dad's. I've got his TT1 Ducati, and the 350cc Offenstadt that he raced in 1975/76. Just like me, Carl said he'd love to get one or two of the old Suzuki RGs or Yamaha TZs from his dad's heyday. It seems that even though we had very different relationships with our Dads, we have both ended up having a lot of respect for them.

12
Friends Reunited

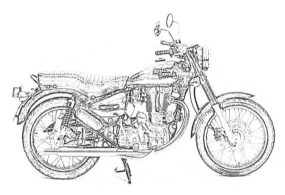

After Dad tried to come back to racing in 1987, two years after his accident in Montjuic Park, he finally gave up in 1991. He spent the four years in between racing mostly his Suzuki GSX-R750 at the TT, but he did also do some racing on short circuits because then, as now, you have to have completed a certain number of races on short circuits in order to be granted a 'Mountain Licence', which is a special race licence you need to race at the TT. He was a physical wreck and really shouldn't have been able to race, but he loved the TT so much that I think it went beyond just wanting to race there again; he needed to race there.

The last time he raced at the TT before the accident in 1985, he won the F2 race, finished second in the F1 race and third in the Production 750 race. In his return to the TT his best finish was thirty-second in the F2 race, on a Honda CBR600. It must have been torture for him because I'm sure he believed that he could just pick up where he left off, and yet he was nowhere. 1988 was worse still, with a best finish of thirty-seventh. In 1989 he managed a twelfth in the Supersport 400 class, riding my Suzuki RGV250 that I was using to start club racing at the time. Looking back, that twelfth-place finish probably rates up there as one of the best rides of his career, purely due to how much of a mess he was physically.

In 1990 he raced a bike he built using a Harris frame and 750cc Ducati engine similar to the one he used in his F1 bike back in the 1980s. It was a beautiful bike, and I actually got to race it a couple of times when Dad was getting me to experience different types of machinery. He finished twenty-sixth in the Senior TT that year, which would prove to be the last time he took the chequered flag at the TT. In 1991 Dad's Harris/Ducati broke down in the F1 race, and my Suzuki RGV also broke down in the Supersport 400 race, so he retired from both the races he entered that year. It must come to an end for all of us at some point and, as I'm starting to realise, the trick is knowing when that is. In some ways I wish he never tried to come back and had just accepted that his injuries were life-changing; he was miles away from being the racer that he was, and I'm sure that's what made him such a hard person to be around. If he hadn't tried to come back, his TT career would have ended in 1985 with a first, second and third in three races, and he could have spent the rest of his life boring people to death about how he was a TT race-winner the last time he raced there. However, I also get just how big a pull the TT has on racers who have experienced it – it's irresistible.

Sadly, even when Dad accepted that he couldn't be competitive anymore and decided to retire from racing, he was obviously never fully at ease with not being able to race. On the upside, his old mates Bob and Keith reappeared in his life, after they had gone their separate ways when Dad's career took off. By the time Dad had his big accident they hadn't seen him for a while, so as soon as Dad was transported back from Barcelona they popped round to see him and of course they remember him with that frame on his head and his eyes being really badly crossed. The doctors said his eyes would slowly straighten up, and I don't think they came all the way back but they were 100 times better than immediately after the accident, especially after they did some work on the nerves behind them.

Bob and Keith had both kept riding on the road, and maybe it was when Dad sold the Harris/Ducati to a mate of his for £6,000 that he decided to buy himself a bike for the road too. I've seen that the Harris/Ducati has changed hands a few more times since, and I believe it's in France these days. A recent picture of it came up on social media not long ago, and it still looks beautiful. I dread to think what it's worth today; that sort of one-off bike with a hand-built frame fetches big money. Keith and Bob said that Dad bought one of the modern Royal Enfields because they had one too; this would have been around 2005/06. When I say 'modern', what I actually mean is one built around the time he bought it. The design and engineering is basically the same as it was back in the day, when they were teenagers, so from a technology point of view there's nothing modern about it at all.

Soon after, Dad got invited to do a parade lap at the TT on one of his Yamahas, but he told Bob that he wasn't going to ride over or take the ferry, and that he'd go if he could fly over. That's what Dad was like, plus he wasn't going to spend money on tickets for the aeroplane, so Bob said they'd pay for the aeroplane if Dad organised the transport over there, which he said he would. When the day came, and the aeroplane landed at Ronaldsway

Airport on the Isle of Man, Bob asked Dad how they were getting from there to the house that they were staying in, ten miles away. Dad just said, 'I dunno, the car isn't here', which is another way of saying he hadn't arranged anything. Meanwhile, Bill Smith, another TT legend, was there picking up John Rudge, who's another TT racer from the 1960's, and his wife. Just as he was always able to do, Dad managed to get Bill to offer him and Bob a lift, so bold as brass, Dad jumped in the front with Bill Smith and left John and his wife to squeeze into the back of the car with Bob. Next thing, Bill says, 'C'mon, we'll do a lap of the course before we go anywhere', and there he was, taking racing lines on every bend, cutting cars up here and there and having a great time. Some things just don't change.

Eventually they got to their accommodation, a lovely bungalow that was immaculate inside and out, with a beautiful cream carpet throughout. They went to their room and Dad decided to polish his shoes before they went out, but obviously he didn't do a very good job because as they were heading out, Dad left a perfect outline of his footsteps across the carpet, which they did their best to remove without letting on to the owner. They had literally been on the island for a couple of hours and were causing all sorts of chaos from the moment they got off the plane.

Dad did organise a car via Kenny Irons, who was another racer, who told Dad that it was parked up in the paddock. When they got there, the only thing there was a tatty old Datsun with the keys in it, so Dad jumped in, started it up and off they went. No sooner had they set off than the exhaust fell off and started dragging on the floor, and then it started raining and the wipers didn't work, plus there was also no tax or MOT on it. Eventually, and predictably, they got pulled over by a policeman and told to get it sorted, but all they did was go to the B&Q DIY shop, which just happened to be next to where the policeman had pulled them over. They made a quick fix to the exhaust, then just dumped the car back where they found it and left.

When it was time to do the parade lap Dad got on the Yamaha that they'd lined up for him. He noticed that the fuel tank had been filled to the brim, but he said that he didn't need that much fuel and made the guys get a bottle and started draining some fuel out of the tank, telling them to take more and more fuel out until he was happy. Everyone completed the parade lap that day except Dad, because he ran out of petrol at Union Mills, which can't be more than a handful of miles into the lap. Bloody parents! For the life of me I don't know what he was thinking by draining so much fuel especially as it was just a parade lap, but I guess old habits die hard.

A couple of years later Mum and Bob's wife Linda wanted to come over for the TT. Bob was over there already to do some trial riding with a local bloke who'd offered the loan of his wife's car so the two couples could go out while over there. The four of them got dressed up to go out and decided to go to the pub in Crosby for a meal. When they got there, Dad took one look at the menu and said there wasn't anything he liked on it, more likely he didn't like that the starters were £12!! and they should go somewhere else. From there, they went to every pub, all the way round the course, and everywhere they went, Dad didn't like the menu, in particular the prices. By 9 p.m. they got to the Creg-Ny-Baa pub, pretty much at the end of the lap. The landlord said they stopped serving food at 9 p.m., but as the group contained Tony Rutter he had something for them, and went out the back. He came back with two T-shirts, one for Dad and one for Bob. They said thanks but that they were starving and really wanted something to eat. So, the landlord disappeared again and back with a bag of crisps and Kit-Kats each for Mum, Dad, Bob and Linda. Dad's reputation for being tight didn't happen by accident!

Keith told me a funny story about when Dad went to buy some cat food from the same place he always did. When he got there, the bloke who owned the shop and had known Dad for a long time told him that the price had gone up something stupid like 50p, and Dad was so disgusted that he put the cat food back and walked out, slamming the door so hard that the glass fell out of it, and they never spoke again. Years later, Dad and Keith were at Oulton Park in the paddock, and Dad spotted the same bloke and his wife walking towards them. He grabbed Keith and made him hide behind a building with him and told him to let him know when they were gone.

One day Dad got some of his trophies down from the loft because they were all knocked about and grubby, and some of the plaques had fallen off, so he took them to a place in Wallsall that could restore them. A couple of weeks later he got the call to say they were all done and ready to collect. When he got there, he got a bill for £200 and Dad spent twenty minutes arguing with the shop, but they didn't budge. I'm pretty sure that because it was his trophies he paid up, but not without making a scene. Then he went back six months later and got more done!

On the subject of Dad embarrassing me, he was a bit of a fussy eater but he did love prawns. At one point I was sponsored by Black Horse Finance, and the bloke who ran it told me that Dad was welcome to go along to their hospitality suite at Brands Hatch as a guest and have something to eat while the racing was on. He went along and started digging into the prawns, and after a while the bloke who was in charge of the food asked the guy from Black Horse Finance who the old man was – the one who was eating all the prawns without taking any of the shells off. The Black Horse Finance guy said, 'That's Tony Rutter, he's a four-time world champion', and just left him there, crunching away on the prawns. When I heard the story, to be fair I wasn't really embarrassed because I found it just as funny as my sponsor did.

In the late 1990s I was racing at Donington Park with Honda, and Ian Simpson and I were sitting in my caravan between sessions. Dad was at the race too; at that time he was still trying to be involved with my career and was coming to all my races, but to be honest by that stage I was in a team so big and with so much expertise that I had plenty of information and advice around me, plus by then he'd already taught me plenty. He walked past, obviously looking for my caravan, and got into the caravan next to us and sat down at the table. We could see him from inside our caravan, but he never saw us. Then we saw him realise he was in the wrong caravan, get up and walk out of it and into mine. He never said a word, and just sat down, completely normal. I asked him where he'd been, and with a straight face he said he'd just been to the garage. I said, 'Anywhere else?' and just started laughing at him until he owned up and laughed along too. He might have been really tight and desperate not to spend money, but he did have a good sense of humour.

Dad also had a fiery temper; he'd say nothing then go mad, especially if he felt wronged by someone. I think it might have been Steve Wynne from Sports Motorcycles who tried to get Dad thrown out a race; he'd put a protest in against Dad for something that obviously just made him snap, and see red. Apparently, Dad searched the paddock for Steve and when found him he threw a toolbox at him. He didn't say a lot but when he did, he meant it. Bob says he can't remember Dad as having a temper; he knew him virtually his whole life and describes him as a sulker for sure but not fiery, so it was probably just me and Steve Wynne that experienced that side of him.

Bob reckons Dad never changed during the time that they went their separate ways for a few years. When Dad finished his racing and bought his road bike, they used to ride to a café and Keith would get a round of teas in, then Bob would get one in then Dad would say he'd had enough and dodge getting a round in, just like they did as teenagers in the pub fifty years before. Something else that never changed was on Wednesdays Dad still had to have a copy of Motorcycle News for his fix of motorbikes, pretty much right up to the end.

I think Dad bought the Enfield to treat himself after he retired, which is fair enough. As soon as he got it, the first people he called were Keith and Bob to tell them to come over because he had a surprise, and there it was: a 500cc Royal Enfield in the garage, and they were all once again back on the road. Two days later Dad was complaining that it was undergeared, which basically means its top speed could be better with different sprockets, so they had to change the front sprocket. Then he was moaning about the carburation, so he got new carbs for it and set them up, but then it was the tyres, they weren't good enough, so he upgraded them. Next it was the oil in the forks that got changed for heavier oil to stiffen the suspension. I remember thinking it's only a Royal Enfield, it's only supposed to be ridden about at a fairly sedate pace to places like the café, and Dad was well into his sixties at this stage. Plus, the roads are different now from how they were then; the traffic is the main difference. When they were teenagers, they used to do the 14 miles from Bridgnorth to Stourbridge in 14 minutes, and I'll tell you now that today that's totally impossible, even though the road is wider and a lot of the bends have been straightened out. The sheer volume of traffic today makes that same journey a 30-minute ride on a good day.

Dad was always fiddling with the Enfield, and he was obsessed with checking if the wheels were perfectly in line. He used a piece of string around the back tyre up to the front to see if they were in line because he swore that using a flat edge like a piece of metal, which is what most people use, could bend or warp. He'd say that nothing is straighter than a taut piece of string. I still check wheel alignment with a piece of string today, just like he showed me, but for Dad, having to have the wheels in line was a massive thing because he would literally spend hours getting them perfectly in line to the last millimetre.

For a few years, Dad, Bob and Keith managed to get about a bit on their bikes, mostly just riding to the café and back for a cuppa, and just like always, there would be some talking point during their ride-outs. One day they were at the café and a lady came over and grabbed Dad from behind and asked if Dad remembered her. Obviously he didn't, so she told him that she was the nurse that tended to him in hospital when he crashed and broke his leg at the TT just before the Gooseneck. Dad and I were regulars at the local hospital with various injuries over the years; I spent time in there from a very young age. I remember falling out of Dad's van into the middle of the road and cracking my skull once – that kept me in hospital for ages.

When Dad was racing his Ducati, someone sabotaged it by putting a coin into the engine via one of the carburettors, so when Dad started the bike the next time, the engine destroyed itself. They found the coin inside the engine when they stripped it down, and the thing is when the bike wasn't being used, there were little covers over the carburettor intake, so they knew it was deliberate because whoever did it would have had to take the cover off the carb to put the coin in, then put the cover back on. It was obviously something that must have been a big deal at the time, because Bob was telling me that one time when they went to the café, Dad started up his bike to come home and they threw some coins on the floor behind the exhaust. They shouted, 'Look, Tony, someone's done it again!' – and there he was in front of the café, having a right sulk. The story reminded me of the time I'd found some ball bearings near where we lived and had put them into a crankcase from one of Dad's bikes that was in the garage at home. I don't know why I did it, but it seemed like a good idea at the time. Blissfully unaware of my actions, they rebuilt the engine and then went to Oulton Park, where it promptly destroyed itself as soon as they started it. Bob and Keith remember that and reckon it was about 1978, so I would have been only five or six years old.

With Dad out and about riding on the road again, he needed a new helmet. He always used to wear Arai helmets at the end of his career, and he was wearing one at the time of his crash. Although it got destroyed, and although Dad had massive head and neck injuries, it probably saved his life. So, Keith took Dad to the Arai distributor to get a new helmet. Dad tried on so many helmets, and he said they were all wrong and that he wanted the same size as me – I wear a medium. The thing is, the size that Dad was trying was a perfect fit, but Dad wasn't having any of it; he had to have a medium. Calm as you like, the bloke who was helping Dad pulled out the helmet lining, telling Dad that he was going to get some special custom lining just for him that would make his helmet a one-off. He disappeared, then came back and told Dad to try it, and Dad declared it perfect. The bloke told Keith that it was the exact same helmet, but he'd just gone out the room and put the very same lining back in. It's another example, like the coins on the floor next to his new Enfield, of how sometimes, but not very often, Dad could be quite gullible. Generally, he didn't suffer fools, but every now and then, especially when he was older, he could be tricked.

The trio of friends would go further afield sometimes, and they went to the bike show at the NEC while they still could. As well as the bikes, I think Dad never lost his appreciation for a pretty lady, and back then female models were still being used by manufacturers to make their bikes look more glamourous. Nowadays it's become an unpopular thing to do, and even in sports like Formula 1, the traditional sponsor's grid girl is no more. Keith and Bob said that Dad was incurable, and for someone who was always quiet and generally kept himself to himself, he had no problem striking up conversations with pretty women, usually by complimenting what they were wearing.

In 2008, not long after Dad got his bike, his health began to suffer, as did that of Barry Randle. Due to standing up in the paper shop for so much of his life, Barry got himself a thrombosis in his leg and ended up having to have it amputated, then the other one had to go too. The racing community decided to do something for Barry, so organised a charity evening to raise money for a wheelchair. Obviously Dad went with his bike, and I went too and brought John McGuinness along; it was a great evening and they raised £3,000 for Barry to buy a wheelchair.

Not long after that, so maybe around 2009, Bob and Keith were getting a bit concerned about Dad going out on his bike – he wasn't really safe – and started suggesting they take the car to the café. It was a shame, but Dad's brain injury was starting to catch up with him; he would say something to me and get stuck halfway through and forget what he wanted to say. He never smoked and wasn't much of a drinker; he preferred to spend his money on petrol, motorbikes and haircuts (when he was younger), but despite that, he was sadly going to suffer from ill health in his later years. Eventually he reached a point when he needed a level of care that neither I, Mum, nor his friends could give, so he had to move into a care home.

As well as Keith and Bob, Dave Burr – who was Dad's big sponsor in the eighties – also became good friends with Dad in his later years. Dave would visit him regularly in the care home and was brilliant with him. On a good day Dad would be about 70% with it, and sometimes you could have a proper conversation. When he wasn't good, I couldn't cope with much more than five minutes, because it was really a one-way conversation with him, and I'm not very good at leading conversations unless it's about bike set-up. I just didn't know what to talk about with him, and to be honest I've probably talked to Dave about more subjects than I did with Dad my whole life. Dave, on the other hand, was brilliant; he's a natural storyteller and he used to be able to get Dad laughing about whatever it was they would talk about that day. The nurses would tell Dave to go and get Dad giggling, because they liked how his face would change when he smiled, even though he was close to death, sitting in a chair and unable to walk or do anything, the nurses would say how pleasant he was. I don't know what it is he had that could do that, but whatever it is, he had it.

The time that Dad spent with his mates after he had finished racing was all too short. Some were his lifelong friends, and others were friends he'd picked up during his life as a racer, and they spent their time just hanging around and doing what they always did. On reflection, this time was a really important part of his story, because the racing paddock will move on and forget you in time, and what are you left with when the racing stops if not your friends?

If he hadn't have tried to come back after his accident and spend four years just going through the motions, frustrated and angry that he wasn't as good as he used to, he would have had more time with them and done more things. It's a real shame, but like literally everything Dad ever did, he did it on his terms, and he might not have always been right, or even nice to people at times, but I do think that reconnecting with his old mates when the racing finished did help him to adjust to life outside of racing.

13
How Did I Get Here?

A t the time of writing this book, the 2021 season is behind us, and I've just started to think about the 2022 season, as the owner of one of the bigger and better-funded teams in the paddock. The North West 200 and TT races are back on the schedule for 2022 again after a two-year absence due to the Covid pandemic, and once again we missed out on the British Superstock title. So, I'm sitting here working out the best thing to do for me, the team and the sponsors, and it occurred to me that sometimes I have no idea how I ended up where I am, and in such a fantastic place, where I have a brilliant sponsor in Bathams, and several others who are just as supportive and passionate about racing that I could pretty much do what I want with the team. It's the dream scenario for anyone, but it does feel like it was only yesterday that I was just like any other bike-mad kid that wasn't keen on school and just wanted to follow my dad about because that was way more interesting.

My mate and I got some tickets for the Saturday at the 1991 British GP because I couldn't afford tickets for race day. Kevin Schwantz was riding, and I was desperate to see him race, so I figured I'd just hide somewhere in the circuit and not go home on Saturday night. That way I wouldn't need to get back into the track on race day if I was already in it. There was a sidecar race team there that I knew through somebody else, and they said I could sleep in their awning, but my mate and I had nothing with us to keep warm, literally just what we were wearing. We needed somewhere warmer and less draughty for the night, so we went to the toilet block that's above the hospitality suites by Redgate corner and I spent the night sitting on the toilet resting my head on the bog roll. It was so cold, but at least we were in the track for race day and got to watch the race. Schwantz won it and threw his helmet into the crowd near to where we were watching from.

I mentioned in *The Life of a Racer* how school and I didn't get along. About the only thing that was any good about school for me was that the playing field backed onto the end of Mum and Dad's garden. It meant that I used to be able to get out of bed at 8.55, not eat anything, go straight out the back door of the house, past Dad's shed at the end of the garden – I remember it used to smell of the old tyres that Dad kept in there – and jump the fence and straight into school in time for the register at 9 a.m.

At school I wasn't the brightest but also not completely stupid. I really struggled with my dyslexia so I thought that if I did Art, it wouldn't involve any writing, just drawing, and anyone can draw. It was a big mistake: there was more writing in art than in any other lesson, and you had to know how to use a pencil and paints. I was so out of my depth and the teacher knew it. Obviously, she knew fairly quickly that I couldn't paint or draw, and that I wasn't that interested in art, so she figured that I joined her lesson for an easy life, which was true. She was so passionate about art, and I think it probably offended her that I was only there to get out of doing something else. One day she made me stand up at the front of the class, and she pointed at a colour and asked me what it was. I said I didn't know, so she told me it was turquoise. Then she asked me what colours are used to make turquoise, which I also didn't know. Then I got a big lecture, and she said that the whole class had to stay behind after school until I found out how to make turquoise. Luckily, there was a girl who sat next to me, and she whispered it to me after about fifteen minutes of pain and humiliation. Not surprisingly, I still don't know what colours you need to make turquoise!

At school I played for the rounders team, and they would make me field miles out because I was good at catching. I remember this bloke hit the ball so hard and so high straight at me that I was thinking it was going to kill me. So, I took my cap off and caught it in my cap, just so I didn't have to use my hands to catch it as I was certain the ball would have broken a bone. I wasn't trying to be flash or anything, just trying to avoid getting hurt. Unbelievably, they didn't allow the catch, so I got more shit for that too.

After I finally left school and got a job at a small dealership called Phil's Motorcycles, I took part in a Youth Training Scheme, which was a government-funded programme that allowed people who left school with no qualifications to learn a trade while getting paid. Sadly, in order to get paid I also had to go to college one day a week and sit in a classroom, which obviously I hated. I would get so bored, but I did enjoy learning to weld at Dudley College; I'd be welding everything I could. Then, after doing some welding, I had to sit and write stuff in a book, which was a complete waste of my life, for a day. There were a few of us who used to mess about, all as thick as each other, and when we were messing about I got my chair and hand up against this tap on the wall, and it just snapped off then water just started gushing out all over the place. I really didn't mean to do it, but it flooded the workshop and classroom, and worst of all, they couldn't turn it off because it was an old building so there was no cut-off valve anywhere in the water system. Needless to say, I got thrown out of the college, and I had to write a letter of apology, that obviously I got someone else to do for me and which got me back in the college a week later. Dad just said I was a bloody idiot. Most kids would have got a right bollocking.

I've always been happy to work hard for my money and take a few risks here and there, even when I was young. I couldn't wait to get a paper round as my first job so I could earn my own money. To be honest, being dyslexic and needing to be able to read the street names on the paper wasn't ideal, so after my first week everyone had the wrong newspapers delivered, and the bloke from the shop got loads of complaints and he went mad at me and said that I had one more chance. The very next day, it was just my luck that there was a massive storm, so the newspapers got soaking wet in the bag, and just by getting them out of the bag they were already wet and destroyed. Fair play to my mum though, she drove to the other newspaper shop up the road, bought all their newspapers and drove me around so I could deliver them from her car. I quit the job the week after; it was a disaster.

Dad also had a motorbike shop for a few years from the late seventies to the early eighties in an area called Quarry Bank. I'd go there at weekends; obviously I would have gone after school if

I could, but it was too far away. He moved to a site in Lye at one point, I assume for a bigger showroom. Mostly Dad left it to people to run; he was more interested in racing. The bike shop was a good idea when Round Oak Steelworks was trading; he couldn't go wrong, so it was relatively easy money for him for a while, I think. The steelworks employed 3,000 people at one point, and even in the 1980s 1,200 people worked there, so when it closed down in 1984, it hit the area really hard. Unemployment hit 25%, which was the highest of anywhere in the UK at the time, and there was already a recession on. Anyone familiar with the area might know of the Merry Hill shopping centre, which is massive. It was built on the old site of the Round Oak Steelworks so it gives a good idea of how big the steelworks were. Inevitably, after the steelworks closed nobody had any money, so the bike dealership eventually had to be closed. I do remember Dad buying TVs to try and encourage people to buy bikes, you know, buy a bike and get a free TV. There was a pile of TVs stacked up in the shop, and looking back it just shows that as well as being a bit of a wheeler-dealer, Dad was also pretty creative at how to get money out of people.

I used to go and hang about in Dad's shop and spend most of my time just sitting on all the bikes, pressing the buttons and controls on them. I'd also head into the workshop and annoy the two guys who worked there, called Guy and Nick. I must have been a nightmare for them, because they would charge up this capacitor with electricity and leave it out for me to pick up, knowing that I wouldn't be able to leave it alone. When I predictably touched the wire, it gave me such a belt of electricity that I thought it was going to blow my hands off. I've no doubt that I deserved it; I was forever messing about with their tools and equipment in the workshop, which for a technician is such a pain in the arse not knowing where your stuff is. They got me loads of times with that capacitor.

People still come up to me today and say they bought a bike from Dad, and I tell them that I apologise! I think his shop was quite popular. In fact, I got a call from a good friend of mine who runs a bike dealership in Preston called Fastline Motorcycles. He called to say that he had taken in a Ducati Pantah 500SL that was originally sold by Dad from the bike shop in the 1980s. It still has the number plate with 'Tony Rutter Motorcycles' on it, and the original paperwork with Dad's handwriting. I just had to buy it, and it's beautiful to ride. It was also a crash-damaged Pantah 500SL that Dad raced at the 1981 TT and won the F2 TT race on, the first of many of Dad's race wins on a Ducati. So, while mine isn't the exact one, it's the same as the first Ducati that Dad raced, plus it's one that he sold from his bike shop, plus I'm its second owner, which is very cool.

Even if I was undoubtedly a pain in the arse at times for Dad, he never had a problem bringing me to his races, and I would go everywhere with him, usually in his Talbot Express van, which I also used when I started out. It wasn't pretty, in fact it was a bit of a heap, but all the same, Dad would drive it flat out everywhere. One time we were driving to Knockhill, in the fast lane of the motorway, when there was a sudden crash and bang, and the bonnet flipped open against the windscreen, blocking the view in all but the narrowest gap at the top of the screen. Dad had to stand up to see through the gap so he could pull over and put a ratchet strap on the bonnet to hold it down.

We used to sleep in the back of that van with a little gas stove to keep warm, which, looking back now, is just mad. At the TT, I'd share the same hotel room with Dad at the Rutland Hotel, which he didn't seem to mind – except maybe for the 1984 TT, when I was sick as a dog, just puking all over the place, and Dad eventually got whatever it was, and he felt like shit for the races.

It's odd, but when I was going through some pictures of Dad for this book, I saw a picture of him riding a Cotton that had a really trick Armstrong engine, and the thing I remember the most about that bike is Dad being stretched out on a table that was in the back of the Talbot Express van – I used to sleep on it during the drive home from wherever we'd been. Every time he rode that bike it would seize up and throw him off, and he'd have to go and lie down and stretch out on that table. Cotton was a small British bike manufacturer from the early 1900s and they were quite revolutionary at the time with their frame designs. Like a lot of the small British bike manufacturers that were around then, they eventually went out of business, so there aren't many of them around now. In fact, there weren't many of them around when Dad raced one in 1980. I'm not sure where he got it from, but I do remember it being different: the radiator was in the nose, so the area behind the front wheel, where the radiator usually is, was all sealed off in the name of aerodynamics. It was quite a cool thing, but the engine was unreliable, so it didn't stay long. That, plus the following year was when he first rode a Ducati – the damaged repaired Pantah 500SL.

Another bike that Dad was keen to get off was the JPS Norton that he raced in 1972. By then he'd won his first British championship, and things were really starting to happen for him. I was born that same year, so I've got no memory of it, and the only thing he ever told me about it was that he was so happy to get a factory ride. Riding for a factory is what we all want as riders. It usually means the budgets are bigger, the resources are bigger and so the bikes are better. He couldn't wait to get on the bike, but he said that straight away it was just horrible to ride, and he never got on with it, and just wanted to get to the end of the contract. It was a big anticlimax for him, and that's all he ever said to me about it. I used to ask Dad about what it was like to race against the likes of Barry Sheene, Mike Hailwood and Mick Grant, and he was always happy to talk to me about that kind of stuff, but he'd never be big-headed about it; he'd just say how good they were.

At one point, Dad was going to build one of those microlite planes, which I think must be the scariest thing I've ever done with him. He used to build and fly model aeroplanes with his friends when he was a kid, so he was well into aeroplanes. We'd been to a show somewhere, and Dad saw this microlite that you could buy as a kit and start building the rear section and work your way through it. He got the tail bit done and, looking back, thank God, he never finished it because we wouldn't be here now if he did. He probably ran out of money or patience; he was one of those that would start a project full of enthusiasm, then something else would catch his eye. I remember going training with Dad when he suddenly decided he wanted to get fit. This was before the accident, so we went running around the block, but he soon got bored with it and didn't do it again. I'm the same. I think with the microlite plane he was basically going up a level and upping the ante from flying his model aeroplanes. I must admit that flying a small plane like that does have a big appeal to me, and one day I really want to fly down the River Severn in something that I've taken off from my back garden in. That would be really cool.

Just like me, there were a couple of key points in Dad's life that took him from a completely normal, average childhood to a life that took him around the world and let him earn a living out of bike racing, and all that comes with it. I think Dad's path crossing with Bob Priest was a significant moment for him. Bob was a bike-racing fan that liked to bet on the horses and was probably looking for ways to avoid the taxman, so backing Dad was a good way to satisfy all three things, and for Dad it was his big break. For me, it was a fella called Barry Reakey from McCulloch who was my first big sponsor, just like Bob was for Dad. Barry used to work for McCulloch and knew Dad from going to his bike shop, and one thing led to another, and the next thing I've got the money to go racing on a Ducati 888, which was my first competitive bike.

You need someone to get you going, someone with money and a common interest and, as in my case, when my career stalled in 2009 after I quit the Yamaha team because I was scared to ride the then-new R1 at the TT. I got lucky again when I was, yes, you guessed it, in the pub drinking a pint of Bathams beer with Dad. What happened next is all explained in *The Life of a Racer*. Dad used to love his Bathams; he was always having a Bathams long before I was old enough, so it's really cool that they've become such a big part of my career. They've done massive things for me.

I found a scrapbook that Dad kept various newspaper clippings in. He was quite good at cutting out stuff and took his time to get the details right. He used to do it for me too when I started. He's got the newspaper article about when he beat John Cooper; it must have been a big thing to beat John because there are lots of cut-outs of that race. There's also the article that *Motorcycle News* wrote about when he did his first 100mph in 1972, which was actually a front-cover story for them. Doing a 100mph lap back then was massive, just like us doing 130mph today. He had all that cool stuff in there, and then there's a load of football stickers in amongst all his clippings, which I've obviously put there although I don't remember. He must have been livid with me!

There were also a couple of other cool pictures that he liked, and these take me back to the time when I was there watching him. There's one of the posts that used to be in the grassed area behind the TT grandstand; that was where parc fermé was, and the posts were to lean your bike against immediately after the race until a certain time had passed, to allow anyone to lodge a protest if they wanted to. No one can touch the bike once it's in parc fermé. There's also a picture of Dad at Donington Park; granted, there are hundreds of those, but the one that he's kept is a picture from the race that they used the footage from in the opening credits of the film *Silver Dream Racer*.

Then, of course, somewhere along the way, Dad and his sponsor Dave ended up being offered to buy Ducati for £1! Thank goodness Dave had the sense to take the advice from the guy at Ducati to not touch it with a bargepole, and luckily the Castiglioni brothers bought it instead. It's just another example of the mad things that happen along the way and that don't really register too much at the time, because as a racer you're so focused on just the racing. I find it hard to believe that I went from once upon a time, when I was about eight years old, getting threatened at knifepoint by some bloke who wanted my pushbike, to years later getting roped into playing in a game of cricket at Goodwood with the commentating legend Murray Walker umpiring. How random is that? I really hate cricket, but at one point I was batting with the TV chef James Martin and Murray had some amazing racing stories. He was so knowledgeable about Dad, and even my racing, which really surprised me. He was a lot like Fred Clarke, who has commentated on motorcycle racing since forever and has such a distinctive voice, just like Murray. Sadly, Murray passed away not very long ago, and Fred has retired now; both will be really missed by the fans of motorsport. Oh, and I just rode away from the bloke with the knife, in case you're wondering, and kept my pushbike a little while longer.

So here I am today, age fifty, looking at the 2022 season, and by the time this book comes out I'll be just about to start my seventy-third TT race, and to be honest, I can't wait. Finally, there's some certainty about the race season after the 2020 and 2021 TTs didn't happen due to Covid, and even the British championships weren't what anyone could ever have imagined. There were no fans for most of the two seasons, and the schedule was crammed into a much shorter space of time, which meant that I, like everyone else, spent a lot more time at home than normal. It has been good and made me see that not everything is about racing and that there are other things; it's given me a different perspective.

2020 with Richard Cooper was meant to be a dream team; I was still doing a bit of racing to try and develop the bike alongside him. Richard was just fantastic and fitted straight into the team and brought a lot of his experience, as well as fresh motivation and a new goal for us all. Unfortunately, he had a big crash at the first race through no fault of his own. I think as a team we didn't give him the best bike, which will always be in the back of my mind; we could have done better for him. I'm a racer, and I think I know our best wasn't good enough. We tried to get help from people who we thought would help, but when it mattered, the bike wasn't good enough for someone of his standard. Dan Linfoot became available to us as a replacement for Richard towards the end of the year, and he got the bike on the podium at the final round. We didn't get a win that year, and Dan's podium was our only one. It was a really hard season for the whole team, but we got back up there at the end.

Taylor Mackenzie came back to us for 2021, and we thought, 'Let's throw everything at it again.' We started the season really well with some wins, then lost our way with the bike, then got back on track with it again at the end of the season, but it was too late to win the championship. The big lesson for me was that it's so difficult running a team because you don't get any of the enjoyment. Even if you win you just get a big bill to pay for tyres, fuel and running costs. Bathams Racing is lucky that we've got amazing sponsors, but it's soul-destroying when you look at all those people watching the racing who have paid to be there, and we're also paying to be there. It costs a massive amount of money for us to put a show on for spectators to then pay and watch. The cost to run Taylor's bike for just one race weekend is about £1,800 for tyres, £200 for fuel, £300 for brake pads, plus the cost of staff, all on top of the £4,500 entry for the season and insurance for the year. We must spend £5000–£6,000 per weekend to run Taylor, not including the cost of the bikes, spares, truck or any crash damage. It's eye-watering, and spending that amount of money to put on a show that spectators also pay to watch has taken all the fun out of it for me. I think if we'd done some road racing as well during those two years I might feel differently because I get a lot of pleasure from that. So, I've decided that we need to take a break from the British championship and start enjoying ourselves again. We're just going to do the things we know we enjoy, so road racing plus stuff like the Classic TT, and I'd like to go back to race in Frohberg in Germany and Imatra in Finland again.

It's hard to think more than half a season ahead at the moment; we'll get through the TT and see where we are then. BSB is the place to be if you want to be British champions, and that still eludes us. It's run brilliantly and it looks great from the outside, but as a team manager or anyone running a team, it's very difficult especially when you've been brought up through the eras when you got paid and tyre companies paid you because they were in competition, and it wasn't a single-tyre rule, so a lot of the costs were met by the organiser and suppliers. I know it's a different era and things move on, but there was also more variety twenty years ago; you could go and do a WSB wild card if you wanted, but now it's just that one bubble, that one format, and it's just week in, week out with the same thing.

When Taylor announced that he was retiring at the end of the 2021 season, I genuinely understood where he was coming from; he did the right thing for him. We've all been at that point and been through what he went through. If he's got something else in his life that he enjoys more, he should do that. There needs to be a balance, and that's why I'm not taking the team back to the BSB paddock in 2022 – I just didn't enjoy it as an owner. You've got to enjoy it. It's too dangerous to do if you don't enjoy it, and there has to be an upside to the risk. In 2007, when I was riding for Kawasaki, I got very close to doing what Taylor has done. I didn't feel well that year generally, and I developed tinnitus and could easily have quit then. The thing that saved me was that I had road racing as a relief. I had a diabolical BSB season that year, then pulled something out of the bag while road racing and enjoyed it again. As soon as you stand on the podium you forget the bad days. Taylor made his decision well before he did that incredible race from thirty-first on the grid to first place at Donington, so I think mentally he was well past that point when a win or podium would reset everything for him. He'd been living with the decision probably before that season even started. Plus the money just isn't in it for riders like it should be, unless you're at the very front of the Superbike class. We couldn't pay Taylor enough, and that makes me feel bad because I think every single rider out there should get paid something at that level. We couldn't pay him and also give him the best bike with all the best stuff; we couldn't do both.

If the past couple of seasons has taught me anything, it's that I have no idea what the next season has in store, and most of all it's important to enjoy what you're doing, otherwise there's no point. That almost makes me sound like an adult, which leaves me wondering just how the hell that happened.

14
A State of Mind

It was something that Trevor Nation said to me that amongst other things really stood out as blindingly obvious, yet only when someone spells it out. He said that comparing racing and racers from different eras is pointless because everyone is going flat out. Riders don't know how good bikes are today compared to before about the year 2000. People might say that today's racers are faster and fitter, but the thing is, everyone who ever raced is going as fast as they can – even the guys in last place are riding as fast as they possibly can. I get it when a youngster looks at me like I'm some old git that used to win a lot of races once upon a time, and I suppose I am, but in my heart I'm still a racer just as much as the next person, who might be half my age. When all is said and done, all racers are the same, past, present, future, young or old. As soon as you line up on a grid, the thing that's inside us, the thing that's brought us to that place, is the same, whether you're Valentino Rossi, Marc Marquez, Mike Hailwood, Giacomo Agostini or the bloke who's last on the results sheet of a club race you'll never hear of.

Going as fast as you can is a drug, and it takes over, especially if you become competitive, which means it intensifies and the only thing that matters is going faster. Again, Trevor Nation summed it up well when he said that he never really thought much about who he was racing against, he just did his own thing. For him, it was always about what he could do on his bike on that day, which is why nobody ever fazed him. He reckons that approach really helped him, because sitting on the start line with your heart ticking over slowly instead of beating fast means you can make sensible decisions. He stopped racing in 1992, and the last time he went to the TT he was on a Ducati that he describes as shit because it only did 150mph on the Sulby straight, whereas his 1985 Suzuki GSX-R was good for 165mph. For 99% of the population, doing 150mph on a normal public road (closed of course) would be madness, but for someone who races at the TT it's not nearly fast enough. These days the Sulby straight is the fastest part of the TT course, so we're nudging 200mph there on the superbikes.

Trevor was sixth-fastest on his third-ever lap of the TT course, then he crashed on the fourth lap, which I think says more about how keen he was, just like we all are, to just go as fast as we think we can, as soon as we can. He managed to stay on the bike, but the impact was so hard that he bent the swingarm and broke the front wheel. He was on the podium once with Dad at the 1984 TT and raced an F2 Ducati similar to Dad's. All he had to say about the bike was that going up the mountain he'd have to wring the neck off it because he had to set the gearing for the much higher top speeds that you get coming back down the mountain towards Douglas. It meant that fifth gear was all the bike could pull going

Dad at the same spot on the TT course (Ballaugh) 20 years apart.

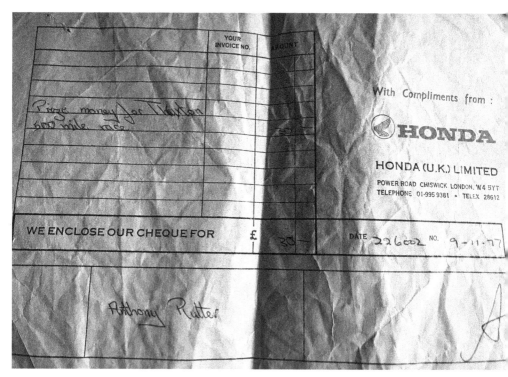

Some gearing settings and £30 prize money receipt I found when clearing out mum and dads house.

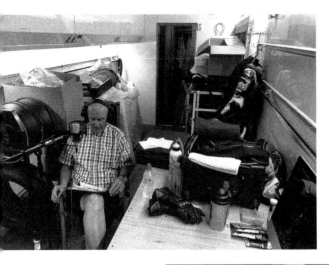

Legendary race commentator Fred Clarke recording the introduction to the audiobook version of *"The Life of a Racer"* in the back of our race truck.

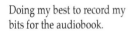

Doing my best to record my bits for the audiobook.

They really went to town in Macau when *"The Life of a Racer"* came out. There was a lot of interest in it.

The Ducati 500SL Pantah that I bought which was originally sold by dad when he had a bike shop.

I love the Goodwood Revival.

Dad in the microlite that thankfully he never finished building.

Carl Fogarty's first race bike came from dad.

ving a bar with Bathams beer in the garage at races is great once the work is done.

Dan Linfoot stepped in after Richard Cooper injured himself and worked hard to salvage the season for us with a podium at the final round.

Me paying Taylor Mackenzie the £1000 that I lost when I bet him he couldn't win from 31st on the grid.

It was one of the most incredible rides I've ever seen.

aftermath of Richard Coopers dent that finished our 2020 on before it started.

Some of my trophies and motorbikes.

Some of my tributes to dad since he passed away that a lot of people including
Fred Clarke who also commentated on many of dads races really liked.

Juliette and Cecillia.

up the mountain, so it felt really slow. The chance to be on equal machinery then was much greater, because of the electronics on today's bikes. It's so easy to get lost with the electronics, and as we discovered, much to our loss in 2021 with Bathams Racing, if you take a wrong turn with the electronics, you're nowhere, even if you've got all the power in the world and one of the fastest riders on the grid. The bikes in Dad's and Trevor's day were a lot slower, but they were terrible round corners, which meant a good rider who understood suspension could make a difference. Joey Dunlop could set up suspension better than anyone in that era, plus he had a sixth sense that somehow let him see around corners, so he was the perfect rider at the time.

These days Trevor rides a Suzuki GSX-R1000 when he's instructing at track days, and even though he's in his sixties now, listening to him describe how he finds the GSX-R and the things he likes about it is like listening to Taylor Mackenzie or Richard Cooper; his feedback is so detailed and precise. The big thing for him is how a modern bike turns, and how you've literally just got to think about it to go round the corner, and how, even on corners with adverse camber, how well the tyre grips. It's thirty years since he raced, but it might as well have been yesterday.

I'm at the stage where I'm happy to race anything because for me it's still about getting that buzz from riding on the limit regardless of what bike it is. I raced a Velocette at Goodwood once with this guy called Michael Russell, and the bike is basically a shopping bike that has been converted into a race bike. It's fast but doesn't handle, and after I rode it in practice for the first time it was a bit scary, because I could see the front wheel flexing a couple of inches in all directions and I thought it wasn't going to end well. We raced it anyway and were actually leading the race when I came in to hand over to Michael, then three laps later the

173

whole of the front end snapped off as he was going through the chicane! I like the Goodwood race; it's got pretty competitive now, so nobody is there parading around.

I also got to ride this Yamaha FJ1200 at the Classic TT, and a bloke called Roger Winfield, who got me the ride, asked if I'd like to do the Philip Island Classic in Australia. I thought it would be brilliant, but it was a nightmare from the start. I got about three laps on the bike before the clutch lever fell off, which wasn't a massive problem, and I planned to come into the pits to get it put back on. Then, at the last minute just as I was coming up to the pit entry, I thought I'd do another lap to check the rest of the bike out because it had just been built. Just as I made that decision, someone on a Suzuki RG500 came past at full speed and clipped my handlebar, causing me to highside in the really fast corner that leads onto the start/finish straight. The bike got smashed to pieces and I took a battering too. Fair play to Roger and the lads, they rebuilt it and got me out in the next session, but from then on, every time I changed gear I got electrocuted with a proper belt from the coil pack. I'd pull into the garage and say, 'The bastard has just bit me again', and they would just laugh at me. It was something shorting when I put my foot on the gear lever, and I was getting properly electrocuted every time I changed gear during qualifying. They found the fault for the race, but even though it hurt like hell there was no way I wasn't going to have a good go in qualifying. It's just what we do.

Fred Hagley said that at some point he was with Dad over at John Hackett's place. John was a great racer in his day and now runs a Ducati dealership in Coventry, and the story goes that Dad went off to talk to someone else and John said to Fred, 'He's a hard bastard', and he could remember at a race at Oulton Park when Dad passed John and knocked him onto the grass. After the race

John started asking around who number 32 was, and someone said, 'That's him over there. I think his name is Rutter', so John went over to Dad and asked him what he was playing at, pushing people onto the grass, and Dad just said, 'Fucking racing', which summed him up well. On the subject of taking to the grass, Dad was leading a race at Aberdare Park once, which is a small road race in Wales that still happens today, and a fella called Jack Gow was behind him. Jack raced a Triumph, and no one ever beat him at Aberdare Park, but he just couldn't get past Dad, so in the end rode through a flower bed to get in front!

Because we're all wired the same, there will inevitably be conflict at some point. When Josh Brookes took me out at Cadwell Park and ruined my chances of the BSB title that year, I thought he was an arrogant prick for the way he was going about his racing; I was just another in a long list of people that he crashed into that season, including five or six in one go at Mallory Park. When a rider does something that's not quite right you're going to be angry, but in time it smooths over because when all is said and done, you're all in the same boat.

However, I think I must be different to other riders when it comes to the things we see and notice when we're out there on the bike, such as braking markers. Once at Thruxton there was this big air balloon for an insurance company that sponsored the series; it was massive, and it was next to the last chicane before the start/finish straight. The braking point is critical because of the very-high-speed approach. During first practice I noticed the balloon was blowing in the wind and moving far enough for me to notice. I just couldn't handle it, so I came in after the first session and asked Stuart Higgs, who runs BSB, if he could arrange to get the balloon moved. He looked at me like I had two heads and asked if I was taking the piss, then lectured me that no one else has moaned about it. I argued that it was distracting me and even though every one of the other riders who I spoke to about it said they hadn't even seen the balloon, they moved it for me eventually. I must have been a factory rider then, because you can pretty much get anything you want when you're a factory rider. Once they moved it I was fine. I must just notice different things to others.

Carl Fogarty wasn't just a factory rider at Ducati: he was, and still is, a god to them, and he told me about the very first time he rode the iconic 916 race bike. He went to Jerez in Spain with James Witham, Giancarlo Falappa and Fabrizio Pirovano, who were the other factory Ducati riders at the time. They got Carl to concentrate on the outgoing 888 and do some tyre work with it, so he was only let loose on the 916 late in the second day, then the next time was at Donington Park, when Ducati used the first round of the 1994 BSB season as a test, and in contrast to James, Carl didn't really like the 916 very much at first. It was nervous and twitchy, and he didn't like the riding position as much as his old 888. All the same, the combination of the 916 and Carl and James meant they won both races. I finished third, and that was pretty much their pre-season testing done with the brand new bike.

They got through the first couple of rounds of World Superbikes with a couple of wins, but Carl was still not convinced that the 916 was any better than his 888, so they went testing at Mugello. There was a prototype with a longer swing arm and different geometry at the front of the bike to slow down the steering at Carls request. No matter how hard he tried, Carl couldn't lap any faster than a 1 minute 57 seconds on his race bike, then Doug Chandler, who was a Grand Prix rider at the time, took the same bike out and did a 1 minute 56.8 seconds. Carl was gutted and couldn't work out how Doug was faster than him on his bike. It's about the worst thing that can happen to you as a racer, when someone takes your bike and goes faster than you on it. Then Carl took the prototype out and reeled off a load of 1 minute 55 second laps, which is still fast today and would have qualified him in seventh for the Grand Prix at Mugello that year. He asked for a slower-steering bike with more stability, and Ducati built one for him, and then he started winning straight away, then the whole Fogarty / Ducati love affair started with probably some of the most iconic races and photos of him and Ducati still to this day. But most of all, I loved his recollection of when he first saw the 916 in his garage at Donington, all done in his colours and with his race number. He also describes it as a stunning bike, the likes of which he, like everyone else, had never seen before, and there was a part of him that was thinking that he didn't want to race it just in case he crashed it.

I was told by Mick Boddice that he and Dad were the first people to ride around Donington Park in 1976, when they finished building it in its current layout. The original layout was quite different to how it is today, so there were a few solo and sidecar racers invited to go and try the new version. Mick was a sidecar racer from Kidderminster and started racing around the same time as Dad, so it was inevitable that they would become friends, just as I became friends with his son (imaginatively called Mick Boddice Jnr) in later years. Mick Snr is still to this day one of the most successful sidecar racers at the TT. It was a month before they opened the circuit, so it wasn't completely finished and the last corner didn't have any tarmac, but I still think it's quite cool that Dad was one of the very first people to ride the current layout. Dad asked Mick if he could have a go in the sidecar, and afterwards he said that he'd never do it again, even if Mick paid him!

Mick and Dad first met at a hotel on the Isle of Man when I was three or four years old, and Mick describes me as a 'right bastard' because I was jumping on all the tables and chairs and wouldn't behave myself. He reckons that if I'd been his, he'd have given me a good thrashing, but basically the first time Mick met Dad was when he went over to Dad to complain about me, and he's spent the rest of his life doing the same, especially when I dated his daughter. He jokes that when I moved in, he and the rest of the family wanted to move out.

My first TT was in 1994, as was Mick Jnr's, so I used to go round to his house and we'd try to learn the TT course by watching the onboard lap that Joey Dunlop did for the film *V-Four Victory*. Obviously, when we got there, it looked nothing like in the film, so we decided to just do laps in a car around the course, and that was a waste of time too because we were just chatting the whole way. Then we got put in a car with Steve Hislop for a lap, and that was brilliant because he kept smacking the mirror with his hand and there were fingerprints all over the windscreen because he was so animated. It stuck in my head because hands were flying everywhere. I'll also never forget that lap because we were taking the piss out of Steve and made him buy the drinks at the Creg-Ny-Baa pub at the end of the lap.

Learning the TT course as quickly as possible was the most important thing in the early days, not necessarily from a safety point of view but because going fast is always the priority. When it came down to it, all the videos and even the lap in a car with Steve Hislop weren't a substitute for actually being out there on a closed road on my race bike. The dominant thought during that learning phase is 'How can I do this section faster?' When all is said and done, even though we all know the TT course is properly dangerous, the way we approach it is the same – to go faster on every lap. Now when I hear riders saying they're going to do the TT, I do fear for their safety. When Josh Brookes announced that he was going to do the TT in 2013, I'm sure he approached it in much the same way he did when he had to learn the UK tracks when he moved here from Australia; he learned the course so he could go fast, which he did to great effect by becoming the fastest-ever newcomer with a lap of 127.7mph, which stood until Peter Hickman came along and made his debut.

The downside to this obsession is that because bike racers have just one thing on their mind, they're actually quite boring. They're not being rude; they just can't hold a conversation about something that isn't about them or bike racing. Dave Burr was saying to me that on the tribute they did to Joey after he died in Estonia, Phil McCallen (he thinks it was him anyway) told him that if you went with Joey on one of his trips to Eastern Europe, you'd get in the van and say hello, and Joey would say hello, and that's all you'd get for the next 2,000 miles, not another word. Granted, Joey was known for being a man of few words, and I had my own experience of that after the Senior TT in 2000, when we had a really good battle on the road. Immediately after the race I wasn't sure if he had the hump with me because I'd put some hard moves on him, and he didn't really say anything to me on the podium, so I really wasn't sure. Then in the press conference a bit later he came over with a beer for me and said he really enjoyed the race that we had, and we sat and drank together. Pure magic.

Roger Marshall has been Riders' Representative and on the judicial panel for British Superbikes for some years but recently took on a role with Yamaha as an ambassador for the Junior Supersport series, which is aimed purely at youngsters as a way into the sport at a high standard. The bikes are up to 400cc machines that produce about 50bhp, so we're not talking about bikes that cost a fortune to buy or run, and the emphasis is on the rider. Yamaha wants Roger to coach the riders, some of which are as young as fourteen or fifteen years old, and pass on his experience to them to try and save them a lot of pitfalls. It's interesting listening to his observations on a lot of the youngsters and their mindsets: a lot of them just want to race somebody they don't like, and he spends most of his time trying to get them focused on doing their own race and riding. He also finds himself having to deal with their parents, as much if not more than the riders themselves, especially in race control, when they start making it all about them. He tries to get the youngsters focused on just racing, as that's the only way you get faster. I don't ever remember having that problem, but I guess that's one advantage of having a dad that raced at his level – he's worked out what's important and the things that will make you faster, which at the end of the day is all that matters. But try telling that to a fourteen-year-old or parent with an axe to grind.

The signs that Dad would probably make a decent racer were all there; I heard loads of stories about how hard he used to ride on the road before he took up racing. I was the same, but oddly enough once I started racing I became a bit of a plodder on the road. It sounds like Dad used to just go flat out everywhere all the time. I'm told by Keith and Bob that they would go to a café that was next to a petrol station, and on one occasion as they were approaching it, Dad was giving it some on his Norton Dominator – Keith on the back, putting the time as the late 1950s. Apparently, Dad was doing about 80 or 90mph past a line of traffic when the car at the front decided to turn right. Dad hit the brakes, then hit a white line, which locked the front tyre and down he went. When they came to a standstill Keith was laying there in the gutter and Dad was trapped under his bike, shouting at Keith to get up and pick the bike up off him, like it was the most normal thing in the world.

On another occasion, Keith told me that Dad wanted to get a new carburettor for a sprint that was coming up at Prees Heath. He had to go to Bandbridge to get it, and Dad and another mate called John Richardson borrowed Keith's bike for the trip because it had two seats. On the way back, he leaned Keith's bike over too far, because Dad had been used to the higher footrest position on his own bike, and the lower footrest of Keith's bike dug into the tarmac and they crashed. Dad went bouncing down into a ditch, complete with a rucksack containing the carburettor. When John eventually found Dad in the ditch, he went over to him in a bit of a panic and kicked him to hurry him up, because the bike didn't have any tax or insurance and they needed to get back without any contact with the police. Years later, Keith and John were talking to Dad, and he mentioned that he'd been for an X-ray that day and that the doctor noticed that Dad had fractured his pelvis at some point in the past. Dad told them that was adamant it was from that accident. Absolute nutters!

Despite mishaps on the road, Dad had a reputation for being a really smooth rider who rarely crashed, and I suppose I've picked up the same 'smooth rider' reputation over the years. It was, in my opinion Ryuichi Kiyonari who redefined the best way to ride a modern superbike, by fundamentally slowing it down a bit more at the apex of the corner, then getting on the throttle much earlier and much harder than my more flowing style which carries more speed into and through the corner but not so much on the exit. I think it's a style that comes from road racing because at places like the North West 200 and TT you've got to be smooth, flowing and pinpoint-accurate.

When Roger did his first North West 200 Dad was at his peak there, and Roger said that he'd been following Dad's career for some time by then so knew that Dad was the man round there and would be good to follow. However, when it came to it he just wasn't in the same league as Dad on the roads at the time. He said that Dad was exceptional on all circuits, road and short circuit, and whatever the bike he was always there at the front. He remembers Dad had a nasty accident at the TT just after Waterworks. It was 1978, which was Roger's first TT as well as Mike Hailwood's comeback year, and Roger remembers thinking how unusual it was to see Dad on the floor because he was so natural, but we all make mistakes. Because Dad broke his leg in practice in 1978, he didn't get to race against Hailwood in his comeback year, but the year after he did, and he finished second to him in the Senior TT. I remember Dad saying that finishing second to Hailwood was his best-ever race at the TT, and that if you gave Mike a hoop and stick to ride that he'd still go round faster than everyone.

Every now and then you have to give best to someone else and just accept they can't be beaten that day, as was the case at the 2019 Macau GP, although as fate would have it I actually came away with a result even I didn't expect. I was there on the Honda RCV and the whole meeting was hard work for some reason. There was a lot of stopping and starting all through practice, not just for us but the cars too; it just never got going. At the start of the race I thought, 'I've got to get in front of Peter Hickman by the first corner', because he was riding the same bike that he had been on all season and he was fastest all through practice and qualifying, and just on another level to everyone else.

I usually get good starts on the RCV so, of course, when it really mattered I made the worst start ever: I think I was third or fourth into turn one, and so I had to get past a couple of people to get on to the back of Peter and hang on to the back of him for as long as I could. However, he was just in a different race on his BMW and he knew what he was doing, so I kept looking to see who was behind me, and I think it was Lee Johnston and Davo Johnson, so I just concentrated on keeping them behind. Then the red flag came out to stop the race because there had been a crash, so we all had to come back into the pits and wait for a restart.

There were more delays while the organisers weren't going to restart it, then they changed their minds and said they would, so we went back on the grid for the restart. This time I thought I couldn't get another shit start, and sure enough I got a brilliant start and got to turn one in the lead with Peter right behind me. Luckily enough, I led for the whole of the first lap and led over the start/finish line at the end of it. By then it was quite late in the evening due to the delays, so the sun had come down and was right in my eyes down into the braking zone for turn one. You're flat out in top gear on the run-down to turn one, and because I couldn't see my braking marker properly I braked way too early, and Peter came past me. He said later that he couldn't see anything either so just used me as a braking marker by just waiting for me to brake, then braked a fraction of a second after me. After he went past, he started pulling away straight away. Then, just as I thought to myself to just forget about Peter, there was a pile-up somewhere behind us that brought out the red flag and the race was stopped again.

The organisers said it was too late to run the race again, and they couldn't run it the following day because of the schedule, so unfortunately it would be declared as a non-event. Then the FIM got involved and decided that because they had stopped the first race, which Peter was leading, that race was null and void. So, by the letter of the FIM law they had to award me with the win because I was leading the restarted race at the end of the last completed lap – which was the first lap. Obviously I didn't want to win it like that – nobody does – and understandably Peter was really upset. He deserved to win because he was quickest in all sessions, set pole position in qualifying and was comfortably leading the first part of the race. I did feel bad about it, so I gave him my prize money, which Dad probably would not have approved of, and I had a go at the FIM people, telling them that it was unfair. All they would say was that's the rules, that how it is, that's the result.

That night, when everything had settled down, I thought about it and realised there have been loads of races during my career that I had in the bag but had lost because things hadn't gone my way. I've been leading races and been passed by people when there's been a yellow flag, which means no overtaking, being shown in one section. You're supposed to give the place back if you do that, but a few times I've been overtaken under a yellow flag and the person has just carried on and won the race. It's unfair sometimes, but then the luck comes your way too, like it did for me at Macau 2019. It will happen to Peter sometime; he'll win some races that he probably shouldn't, I'm sure it balances itself out over time if you do it long enough.

In the heat of the moment it's very hard to console yourself if you feel like you've been robbed of a result; it's the nature of the beast. We are still human, which means we do have a degree of common sense that helps us recognise that even if the history books show that the result on the day was second place, or some bad luck outside your control has affected the outcome, in many ways it's the performance we put in as a racer that we take the most satisfaction from. Dad's best race was when he finished second to Mike Hailwood at in the 1979 Senior TT, and mine was when I finished second to Ian Simpson in the 1998 F1 TT. I've gone faster since then and I've won seven TT races since then, but from a personal performance point of view, and putting together the best four consecutive laps of the TT course, that race was the race of my life – so far.

15
Tributes

After Dad died I got a lot of lovely messages from people who knew him, and there were some very nice obituaries written about him in the motorcycle media, as well as local media. I wrote eulogies for Mum and Dad respectively and I have included them. I really wanted the following pieces to be part of this book. I hope you like them as much as I appreciated them.

Kevin Schwantz

I'm sure I must have met Tony somewhere at some time, but after my career took off, I don't know if I ever got the chance to sit down with him and tell him thank you so much. I never got the opportunity to thank Tony personally for giving me his bike that he'd made so nice to ride. I definitely owe him a very big thank you, and if he was still alive, I would give him a huge hug.

Roger Marshall

I'd like to say what a guy he was. In my eyes he was a complete professional, he had an amazing career and it's such a shame about his accident, because he wasn't a crasher, and everybody said his career was over, but you know it was typical of Tony, that steely determination that got him back. I can remember at the TT, I think it was the 750 Suzuki, a blue and white one, and I remember seeing him struggle to get on that bike with his injuries, and he went out on it on the first night and put a decent lap in on it, and I thought what a bloke. Everyone had written him off and he came back and did that. I can remember it like it was yesterday. Watching him walk and watching him get on that bike I thought that is typical Tony.

When he retired, I kept in touch on the phone a bit and I saw him at meetings. I took an interest when Michael started, and eventually helped him a little bit with his early days. I remember after I had my hips replaced, Michael was at his wits' end and asked me to ring his dad to try and get him to have his hips done. I didn't start the conversation on operations until eventually I got him to come round to asking how I was. Then I was able to tell him that I'd had both my hips done and how well it had gone and how good I was walking. Typical Tony, you couldn't tell him anything, you had to trick him to make him think he thought of it, but typical Tony, he took it all in and he obviously decided against it again; he was set in his ways.

I was so sorry that we couldn't give him a good send-off and have a lot of ale together, but one day I think we should have a party and a toast for him. I was one of the lucky ones to know him, and to see his amazing talent.

George Fogarty

We knew each other for twenty years, and Tony loved the TT, the North West 200, the Ulster GP, Oulton Park and Cadwell Park. He was a legend, but not known as a legend.

Trevor Nation

Tony and me raced Ducatis together for a bit. I raced for Sports Motorcycles, and quite often we'd be in the same race so there was a bit of rivalry to be the best Ducati. We always said hello, but I really kept myself to myself, I didn't really socialise with anyone, but I remember talking to Tony and always had nice conversations with him. He was highly respected in the paddock and fought as hard behind the handlebars as anyone these days.

'TT Legend Tony Rutter has Died'

iomttraces.com

One of the finest Isle of Man TT racers of his generation, Rutter began his TT career in 1965 and would go on to amass 20 podiums and 7 victories around the TT Mountain Course.

Born in 1941, Rutter started racing at the age of 20 and graduated to the TT aged 23 when he contested the Junior Race and finished 46th.

The Brierley Hill rider soon climbed up the leaderboard, placing 13th and 14th in the Junior Races of 1968 and 1969 respectively before taking his first major result in 1970 when he placed fifth in the same race.

A first podium came in 1972 when he finished second to the great Giacomo Agostini in the Junior Race, which was also the first of his five World Championship podiums.

The following year saw Rutter make the step up to the top of the podium, claiming his maiden TT win in the Junior Race when riding a 350cc Yamaha backed by Bob Priest, a Stourbridge businessman who had been a loyal supporter of Rutter since 1969.

It kick-started a superb run of success and, along with the likes of Charlie Williams, Mick Grant and John Williams, made Rutter one of the best British riders of the 1970s – not just at the TT but at short circuits across the UK.

A second TT victory on the Priest Yamaha came in the 1974 Junior Race, a year when he also took podiums in the Senior and Formula 750cc races. Three more podiums came in 1976 when he finished second in the Junior and Production races and third in the Classic Race.

Out of luck in 1977 when he had no less than four retirements, the following year was also lean as a rare crash in practice led to a broken leg. But Rutter was back in 1979, finishing second to Mike Hailwood in the Senior Race and setting his fastest ever lap of the TT Mountain Course at an average speed of 112.32mph while riding a Suzuki RG500.

1981 saw Rutter claim the first of four famous Formula Two TT wins with Ducati, with the second coming twelve months later. Indeed, 1982 was a superb year on the island with another victory coming in the 350cc race and a third-place finish in the Classic Race.

Despite being a more senior racer at this stage of his career, Rutter was still a major force to be reckoned with at the TT and two further Formula Two wins came in 1983 and 1985.

But 1985 would be the last of his seven TT victories as, a little over a month later, he was involved in a multi-rider crash at Montjuic circuit, Spain that almost cost him his life.

He recovered enough to ride again, returning to the TT in 1987, and although the injuries sustained meant he couldn't reach his previous heights, Rutter did take 12th place in the 1989 Supersport 400cc Race.

By then, his son Michael had begun his own road racing career and Tony would remain in the paddock for many years to come as he nurtured Michael's considerable talents which, to date, have seen him match his father's achievement of 7 TT wins.

In total, Tony Rutter competed in 83 TT Races, finishing 51 and winning no less than 33 Silver Replicas. His 7 wins and 20 podiums cement him as one of the greatest ever TT racers.

Elsewhere, Rutter recorded five victories at the Ulster Grand Prix and nine wins at the North West 200, which included the only ever dead heat when he shared the 1977 350cc victory with Ray McCullough.

He was also twice British champion, winning the 1971 350cc and 1973 250cc titles, and contested the World Endurance Championship for Honda Britain.

'Tony Rutter – the man who saved Ducati?'
Steve Rose, Bennetts Insurance

Tony Rutter 1941–2020; Seven-times TT winner, four-times world champion and all-round racing good guy remembered.

In among the noisy and more glamorous prima donna heroes of bike racing, there's always been a bunch of hard-working, talented all-rounders. These guys are the guns-for-hire that teams turn to when they need a safe pair of hands to deliver results that are better than their resources should allow. The easy-to-work-with, thinking riders who will bring the bike home and more often than not will finish on the podium too.

You'll rarely see too many fans wearing their hats and T-shirts, but without these heroes, bike racing would be a whole lot less interesting. Tony Rutter was one of the best. He rarely had the quickest bike, but got far better results on whatever he was riding than others would have managed. Rutter was at the opposite end of the 1970s 'playboy racer' spectrum to the Sheenes and Agostinis. He was a grafter and a man who learned how to get the best out of whatever he had and how to bring it home intact.

Simply surviving the IoM TT in the 60s and 70s was achievement enough. Most racers could only dream of a podium or perhaps a victory. Tony Rutter won seven TTs, rarely on the fastest bike and, in the process, he helped keep the Ducati factory alive in the early 1980s.

The Bologna factory, aided by some talented, enthusiastic privateer race teams, had a good 1970s after Paul Smart's achievements on the bevel-drive 750SS racer and Hailwood's legendary TT comeback. But by the early 1980s they were in trouble. Their belt-drive Pantah 600 motor was good … for a twin, but in the showrooms no one was buying twins when the Japanese four-stroke multis and two-stroke screamers were getting faster every year.

In the Formula 2 World Championship, mid-capacity road bike engines were fitted into bespoke racing chassis. Most of the Japanese attention was on the larger capacity Formula 1 racing, which allowed Ducati an opportunity to dominate F2.

Their bikes were tiny, beautiful and handled better than most, but the Japanese-engined bikes were quicker. Rutter, who'd made a name for himself on the UK national circuits throughout the 70s riding 250 and 350cc Yamahas was signed by Ducati. He repaid their faith by winning four F2

World Championships on the trot between 1981 and 1984. He also took four TT wins in five years on the 600 Duke.

Without his success on the 600cc Pantah twin, there would arguably have been no Ducati 851, no 916, no MotoGP bikes and possibly no Ducati as we know it today. His place in the Ducati story is every bit as important as Hailwood, Fogarty, Bayliss and Stoner.

Most of our generation know the Rutter name through the achievements of his son, Michael. Funnily enough Rutter Jr has exactly the same talents as his dad – an uncanny ability to ride pretty much whatever he is given, at a pace few others can match, in all weathers, without complaining. He's not too shabby on the roads either.

Michael's autobiography was released last year and in it he talks about his early years in the road race paddocks and the influence his dad had on his racing. It's a good read simply because the Rutters are some of the good guys in bike racing.

When motorcycle racing resumes at some point in 2020 we at BikeSocial will be cheering Michael on that little bit louder in memory of his dad, because they both deserve it.

Thanks for everything Tony, we'll miss you.

'Obituary: Tony Rutter (1941–2020)'
Phil Wain, *BikeSport News*

Tony Rutter, who passed away on Tuesday morning, was one of the finest British racers of his generation, equally adept on the short circuits as he was the roads, and in a career that spanned almost thirty years, he was a multiple winner wherever he went.

Successful on anything from a 125cc to a 1,000cc Honda, there wasn't a bike Rutter couldn't win on and he was, without doubt, one of Britain's most accomplished, unassuming and, perhaps, underrated riders.

Born in 1941, Rutter started racing at the age of 20, graduating to the TT in 1965 when he contested the Junior race and he competed on the island for the next twenty years with his first podium coming in 1972 when he finished second behind the great Giacomo Agostini in the 1972 Junior, the race also giving him the first of his five World Championship podiums.

That year also saw him have a brief spell with the JPS Norton team but in 1973, it was the 350cc class that saw him claim the first of seven TT wins with victory coming on his Bob Priest-backed Yamaha in the Junior race, Rutter having been loyal to the Stourbridge businessman since 1969.

That started a run of superb success and, along with the likes of Charlie Williams, Mick Grant and John Williams, made Rutter one of the best British riders of the 1970s, at every circuit across the UK.

It didn't matter if it was Mallory Park, Oulton Park or Silverstone, Rutter was amongst the leaders and record breakers at almost every short circuit and this was reflected in his ACU British Championship tally where he won the 1971 350cc and 1973 250cc titles, having previously finished second overall in the former in 1970 and the latter in 1969.

1973 saw him claim the first of his nine North West 200 wins with victory coming in both the 250cc and 350cc races and that year's Ulster Grand Prix also saw him come out on top in the Junior class.

A second TT victory came in the 1974 Junior race, a year when he also took podiums in the Senior and Formula 750cc races, and three more podiums came in 1976 when he finished in second place in the Junior and Production races and third in the Classic.

By now, Rutter was a regular winner at the international road races with further NW200 success coming in 1977 when he not only won the 250cc race but also tied for victory with Ray McCullough in the 350cc encounter, the only dead heat in the history of the event.

His short circuit prowess could be seen regularly during this period too, a leading contender not only in every 250cc and 350cc British Championship race but also on the big four-strokes with Honda Britain signing him to contest the World Endurance Championship in 1977. He also finished fourth overall in the 1978 British Formula One championship whilst riding for the Mocheck-backed team.

After a nine-year spell with Bob Priest, Rutter would go on to be sponsored by some of the sport's greatest enthusiasts including Sid Griffiths and chicken farmer Harold Coppock and it was on the latter's 500cc RG Suzuki that he recorded his quickest lap of the TT course, 112.32mph, on his way to finishing second behind the late, great Mike Hailwood in the 1979 Senior race.

By then, Rutter had come to the attention of the Italian Ducati factory and he would give them no less than four successive World Championships in the Formula Two category from 1981 to 1984. Four TT wins in five years were also taken on the 600cc Ducati.

The wins kept coming, whether on the roads or circuits with 350cc success coming at both the TT and North West 200 in 1982, also using the same 350cc Yamaha to finish, remarkably, third in that year's Classic TT race.

Despite entering the veteran stage of his career, Rutter was still a major force to be reckoned with as podiums were taken at Donington Park in the 1984 and 1985 British Champion-ship races and although the four-stroke era had now come into *the ascendancy, Rutter's versatility continued to serve him well when he rode a GSX-R Suzuki into second and third place, in the 1985 Formula One and Production B TT races respectively.*

That year saw him claim the last of his seven victories and 20 podiums at the TT as, just over a month later, he was involved in a multiple pile-up at Montjuic Park, Spain that almost cost him his life. He recovered enough to compete at the TT again between 1987 and 1991 although the injuries sustained meant he was unable to reach the previous heights.

By then, his son Michael had begun his own road racing career and Tony would remain in the paddock for many years to come as he nurtured Michael's considerable talents which would see him become as equally successful in both the British Championships and at the Isle of Man TT and North West 200.

Rutter's legacy can be seen in his success which saw him win seven Isle of Man TT wins, nine at the North West 200, five at the Ulster Grand Prix and two British Championships as well as countless individual race wins throughout the British Isles.

'Tributes paid to race legend Tony Rutter'
James Driver-Fisher, Express & Star

Tony, who also claimed nine North West 200 wins and two British titles during a stunning 22-year career, passed away peacefully yesterday morning, aged 78.

The much-loved motorbike racer, from Wordsley, in the Black Country, won pretty much every title going during his illustrious career.

His son, Michael, 48, from Bridgnorth, Shropshire, who

equalled his father's seven TT wins last year, said: 'It is with sadness that after a period of poor health, Dad passed away.

'I was with him when he died at about 2am (Tuesday morning) and he was very peaceful.

'It makes me smile how Dad lived his life exactly how he wanted to – and how he got away with so much!

'He will probably be best remembered for winning the world TT-F2 championship four times on a Ducati, as well as seven Isle of Man TT wins, nine North West 200 wins, and two British Championship titles during his 22-year career.

'I'd like to say a big thank you to his carers for taking such good care of him and all his fans and supporters.'

Tony, who ran his own bike garage and would often frequent Quatford Café, near Bridgnorth, in retirement, survived a horror 150mph crash that nearly cost him his life in 1985 when he hit a patch of oil.

It followed a multiple bike pile-up at the Montjuic circuit, in Barcelona, which left Tony in a coma and on a life-support machine for 10 days.

But despite breaking his neck in two places, all the ribs down his right side, smashing his hip, breaking a leg and an arm, and also damaging the nerves in his left eye – after skidding on a patch of oil while riding in a 750cc world championship race – he managed to return to racing two years later, before retiring in 1991.

During his career, Tony raced against the likes of Barry Sheene, Mike Hailwood and Joey Dunlop on the circuits and roads, and in later life even competed against his son, Michael, who followed him into racing and who has himself enjoyed a very successful 30-year career.

'Isle of Man TT race winner Tony Rutter has died'
Josh Close, Motorcycle News

Seven-time Isle of Man TT race winner Tony Rutter has died at the age of 78 following a short illness.

Tony Rutter, father of fellow racer Michael, enjoyed a successful career throughout the 1970s and 1980s.

Alongside his seven TT victories, achieved between 1973 and 1985, he also won nine races at the North West 200. Rutter's 1977 350cc victory is a historic one after he and Ray McCullough crossed the line at the exact same time. This remains the only tie in the history of the event. As a result of his success, Rutter was inducted into the NW200 Hall of Fame.

Rutter also won four consecutive TT Formula Two World Championships for Ducati between 1981 and 1984, and secured two British Championships during his career.

'Racing legend Tony Rutter sadly passes away'
Kyle White, Belfast News Letter

A hugely talented rider, Englishman Rutter made his debut at the Isle of Man TT in 1965 in the Junior race. It was the start of a 20-year association with the world-famous event and he famously finished as the runner-up behind Italian great Giacomo Agostini in the 1972 Junior race to earn a world championship podium, one of five he achieved throughout his career.

His maiden victory around the Mountain Course swiftly followed in the 350cc class in 1973 in the Junior race and he would go on to notch up a total of seven TT triumphs.

Rutter, with his distinctive 'TR' helmet design, quickly

became one of the best-known riders in the UK as he enjoyed a spell of success in the 70s alongside names such as Mick Grant, John Williams and Charlie Williams.

He was a two-time British Champion, winning the 350cc title in 1971 and the 250cc crown in 1973, which was also the year of his first win at the North West 200.

Rutter chalked up a brace in the 250cc and 350cc races and later that year he showed his prowess on the smaller bikes with victory in the Junior race at the Ulster Grand Prix at Dundrod. Another TT win followed in 1974 in the Junior race but Rutter also shone in the premier class as he claimed rostrum results in the Senior and Formula 750cc races.

In 1977, he won the 250cc race at the North West and was famously involved in a dead heat finish in the 350cc race with Northern Ireland's Ray McCullough – the only such result in the history of the international road race.

He set his fastest ever lap of the TT Course in 1979 on a Suzuki RG500 at 112.32mph as he finished second behind Mike 'The Bike' Hailwood.

Rutter was a rider in demand and he was signed by Italian manufacturer Ducati. And how he delivered, winning four world titles in the Formula Two category between 1981 and 1984. He also added to his tally of TT wins, claiming four victories on the 600cc Ducati in a five-year spell.

More success followed at the North West in 1982, where he won the 350cc race before triumphing on the same machine at the TT.

In 1985, Rutter achieved the last of his seven TT wins before he was seriously injured in a crash at Montjuic Park in Spain after a multiple bike pile-up. He recovered and went on to race at the TT again from 1987 until 1991, albeit without ever hitting the same heights.

His son Michael followed in his wheel-tracks to become a highly-successful racer in his own right in the British Championship and at the international road races such as the North West 200 and TT.

Rutter is also the most successful rider ever at the Macau Grand Prix, where he won for a record ninth time in 2019.

Pauline Rutter Eulogy by Michael Rutter

Mum was born and raised right here in the heart of the Black Country and like many who are, she was proud of that fact. She grew up with her brother Peter, and by all accounts led a much more colourful life than she probably expected.

At a time when travelling wasn't as easy as it is today, and the world was a much bigger place, mum got to go to places as far away as America and Japan and as close to home as Ireland with Dad.

She supported Dad's racing through the highs and lows of his career, and it especially can't have been easy for her when Dad suffered major injuries in a crash while racing in Spain to try and keep things as normal as possible for a teenage version of me. But she did.

She may not have been as well known locally as Dad, but within the race paddock she was known and loved by a lot of people, so later on, when my own racing career started to take off and Mum started coming to the races again, I'm sure she enjoyed it. Mum was a very caring person and had a lot of friends who she loved going to Cliff Richard concerts and on holidays with. She also loved cats and at one time had four or five in the house!

I found a collection of family pictures that Mum took, and my two daughters were in a lot of them. She adored her only grandchildren Juliette and Cecillia and used to love having them round when they were toddlers so she could take them for walks at Kinver Edge. Sadly, Mum's later years were affected by poor health, and she moved into a care home. It meant that she didn't get to see her grandchildren, nieces, nephews and friends as much as she might have liked to, but I know that Mum always loved me and cared for me and my kids, even with her illness.

Of course, it is very sad that she has passed away so soon after Dad, but it does seem somehow typical that they shouldn't be apart for too long. Even in later life, watching Mum and Dad in the care home together really brought it home to me how much they genuinely cared for each other.

Having said that, I do remember one time when Dad had been out too late for her liking. She filled a shopping bag full of water and hung it over the door, so that it fell on him when he eventually came home. She was a strong person, and not afraid to let her feelings be known, usually through action not words!!

I'm sure that being the wife and mum of a motorbike racer can't have been easy for her. It's not a normal lifestyle for a family, and rarely works out. Always travelling, always worrying about the safety of Dad then later on me and living with people who are almost always only thinking about racing must have been at times very difficult for her, and maybe a bit lonely. But something inside her was happy to sacrifice her own career so that Dad and then me could chase our own dreams. We, like everyone else that knew her were very lucky to have her in our lives.

Tony Rutter Eulogy by Micheal Rutter

Obviously my earliest memories of Dad all revolve around racing and motorbikes. Wherever he was racing, I went with him because I just wanted to be with him.

His status as a racer never really registered with me until I went to the North West 200 for the first time with him after I left school. The North West always clashed with school, and as much as I'm sure they wanted to, school wouldn't let me go to it on top of the TT and all the British Championship races that Dad took me with him to. When we got there, I couldn't believe how many people all wanted to see him and meet him. It was a shock to me to see how popular he was. I had no idea, probably because he had no idea himself.

Later on, I began to understand that Dad had a reputation for being a tough, stubborn competitor on track. It was a side to him that I only really understood after his crash at Montjuic Park. His neurosurgeon even told me that he'd never seen anyone fight so hard to survive. During his recovery he was in so much pain and must have been so low because it was the only time I ever saw him cry, but he got himself back racing. It's all he ever wanted to do, and fair play to him he did it.

I've always used Dad's design on my race helmet, not because of all his success as a racer, but because he is and always has been my hero.

Tony Rutter Tribute by John McAvoy

It's safe to say that everyone will have far more memories and time spent with Tony over the years than me. I've only really got to know him in the last few years mostly through stories told to me by Michael. We've looked at probably hundreds of photos of Tony, from long before he committed his life to racing, through to his later years before ill health took over. We've also gone through a lot of Tony's possessions and memorabilia such as his trophies, medals, race suits, crash helmets, dog tags, race licences, the 32-litre fuel tank that he bought from Mike Hailwood, his pit board and even his collection of MCNs. We also found Tony's original medical report that was produced by his neurosurgeon Dr Bernard Williams after his accident at Montjuic Park. Most of these things came with a story or a memory attached to it from Michael, and they all had a similar theme: Tony's obsession with racing and winning.

Tony's incredible achievements as a racer are well documented and I am certain you don't need me to highlight them to you, other than to note that they are unlikely to ever be bettered in the sport. It would be negligent of me to not acknowledge Tony's extraordinary racing career that he dedicated and sacrificed so much of his life to.

For anyone to win a short circuit world championship once is extraordinary, to win two is the stuff of fairy tales, but to win four in a row is a once-in-a-generation event. However, to be so dominant on short circuits whilst during the same period record victories at the Isle of Man TT and North West 200 road races unquestionably secures Tony's status as one of the legends of motorcycle racing. It simply cannot be overstated just how big an impact the records that Tony set made to the sport. I don't believe we will see the likes of it ever again.

Researching all the hundreds of photos and video footage of Tony it would have been easy to miss a subtle but recurring theme in them all. Apart from the fact there was rarely ever anyone else in the picture with him (I assume because he was more often than not in the lead), there wasn't any of him doing celebration wheelies, burnouts or fist-pumps. Despite his chosen profession, the showbiz side to motorcycle racing and playing to the crowds didn't seem to sit very well with Tony, something backed up by the tale of him getting his mate Dave Burr to cover for him on radio interviews.

Tony once told me the story about how his helmet design came about. I was mildly disappointed to learn that the simple red and white design had no origins other than to be recognisable from a distance by his competitors. I can't be completely sure, but I really do believe that for Tony, being identified by the fans wasn't his main priority, whereas making sure his competitors knew who they were dealing with was. He knew that his reputation for being a hard racer on track preceded him, and his unique helmet design let him use that reputation to his advantage.

It's safe to say that Michael was Tony's number-one fan, and much to the relief of Michael's schoolteachers, Tony was more than happy to take Michael out of school to go racing with him. Not very long ago, through a chance set of circumstances, Michael and I had the opportunity to visit Scarborough, and the Oliver's Mount course that Tony raced at when Michael was a child. It was a brilliant few hours, and the more we explored the town and the course, the more memories came back to Michael. He found the spot in the paddock where they pitched their caravan, where he used to stand and watch Tony start the races from and where he got the scar on his lip from – it all came back to him. One memory that didn't come back to him was how Tony did in any of the races there, which really confirms that for Michael, going to the races was about just wanting to be around his dad, and given how obsessed Tony was about racing, he must have really wanted Michael there with him too.

It was a thirteen-year-old Michael that Tony turned to when he wanted someone to remove the bolts for some relief from the brace that was attached to his skull supporting his broken neck. Their relationship might not have been a typical father–son one, but there is no question that Tony loved having Michael by his side, and that Michael also wanted to be with Tony, right up to the very end.

It's safe to say that Tony will be missed by many more people than just his friends, the race paddock and Michael. He also leaves behind his wife Pauline who has since also passed away and his two granddaughters Juliette and Cecillia.

The reaction online by fans of the sport all over the world to his passing was huge, which I suspect Tony would have found all a bit embarrassing. What I do know is that more than anything else, Tony wouldn't want us to dwell on his passing, and instead he'd want us to take a leaf out of his book and for us all to get back to doing the things that make us the happiest, whatever that might be.

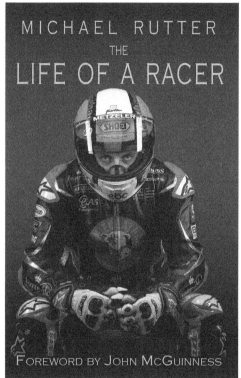

For copies of *The Life of a Racer* and
other "Rutter" merchandise visit

www.michaelrutter200.com

CPSIA information can be obtained
at www.ICGtesting.com
Printed in the USA
BVHW051945070223
658072BV00002B/16

9 781789 632934